BILBREW WRITERS' ANTHOLOGY

Looking Back...
Stories of Resilience
^

Edited by Flo S. Jenkins

Rona S. Cook-White • Odie Hawkins • Ron L. Dowell
Patricia Forté • Jerry Boyd • Zola Salena-Hawkins

Published by Bilbrew Writers' Workshop
Los Angeles, California

Published by Bilbrew Writers' Workshop
Los Angeles, California

Looking Back...Stories of Resilience: Bilbrew Writers' Anthology
Copyright © 2025 Bilbrew Writers' Workshop
ISBN: 979-8-9924462-0-3 (paperback)
ISBN: 979-8-9924462-1-0 (ebook)

First Edition, 2025

Printed in the United States of America.

Cover design by Emily Anne Evans
Layout design by Rona S. White & Emily Anne Evans

This anthology is dedicated to Rose Mitchell, the cocreator of Bilbrew Writers' Workshop and a key contributor to the success of the Black Resource Center.

CONTENTS

INTRODUCTION

Bilbrew Writers' Anthology 2025

Socrates once said, *"An unexamined life is not worth living."* Centuries later, a literary giant, named James Baldwin said, *"Not everything that is faced can be changed, but nothing can be changed until it is faced."* We, the members of the Bilbrew Writers' Workshop support these ideas. We have given you a glimpse into our childhoods in hopes of enlightening the next generation on why we are the adults we are today. We understand that broken parents and caretakers leave 'imprints' on children's vulnerable souls. We are examining our pasts, and in doing so, we trust these reflections will help us change the things in our lives that need changing.

Our stories take us on journeys from the south to the east to the west. One story tells you about an impressionable young boy growing up on the backroads of Alabama, another story takes us to the 'slumghettos' of Chicago where a young boy finds his true passion, while another story allows you to see a family's struggle as they lived on a military base in Port Chicago, California. A young girl in Hackensack, New Jersey, tells us how her middle-class upbringing imprinted her life and made her the woman she is today. A young boy tells us about the ups and downs of growing up in public housing in south central Los Angels, his take on the Watts Rebellion, his bout with drugs and his minor scrapes with the law only to turn his life around and become a productive citizen and an accomplished writer. A young girl in Compton shares the ups and downs of her parent's marriage against the backdrop of some very colorful characters in her family tree.

We trust that the lessons learned and the events experienced will shed some light on the social and political climate that shaped our lives in America. Our timeframe begins in the 1940s and carries into the new millenium.

We are **looking back** in order to **move forward**. These stories are being shared with you in hopes of giving you a better understanding of how we've all been impacted by life in Black America.

Patricia Forté
Bilbrew Writers' Workshop

HISTORY

A.C. Bilbrew Writers' Workshop

The A.C. Bilbrew Writers' Workshop was the brainchild of **Rose Mitchell** and **Odie Hawkins**. Mitchell, a librarian at the Bilbrew Library and head of the **Black Resource Center** there, met with Hawkins — an alumnus of the legendary **Watts Writers' Workshop**. These two discussed the possibility of establishing a Creative Writing Workshop.

The idea floated around a while and eventually became a reality by an exchange of phone numbers between Rose Mitchell, Odie Hawkins, and a lone writer, Patricia Forté. Ms. Forté had been looking for a creative environment to help her with a novel she was writing.

Mr. Hawkins agreed to steer the workshop. He explains, "The basic idea I had in mind of what a writing workshop should be is that a creative environment be established. Some of the people who come into our workshop are dealing with spelling challenges, grammar challenges, and the challenge of telling a coherent story. I don't feel they should be denied the opportunity to have their shot."

Since 2013, the Bilbrew Writers' Workshop has served the community by opening its doors and assisting writers in putting their stories down on paper. It is with great pleasure that we present this anthology for your enjoyment and enlightenment.

If you have a story that needs to be told, and if you have a desire to share your joy, your pain, your culture with others, know that this workshop opens its doors several times a year to new members. We welcome you.

OUR MISSION:

The mission of the Bilbrew Writers' Workshop is to cultivate and respect the voice of individual writers as they explore cultures and bring human experiences to life. We will meet them at the intersection of creativity and passion.

Looking Back...
Stories of Resilience

ONE

THE SHAPING AND RESHAPING OF MY MORALITY

Jerry Boyd

1940's

Ma always said, when I complained about how Whites treated me, "You're not responsible for how they treat you. You're responsible for how you treat them."

GROWING UP IN BARFIELD, ALABAMA

Barfield, Alabama, was a small, rural, segregated town in the 1940s. It had three general stores and one gas station, but no post office, no police station, no bank, and no traffic signals. And to this day, traffic signals in Barfield are still conspicuously missing.

Back then, if you needed to do a simple task like mailing a package or picking up a bulky item from the post office, you would have to travel to the neighboring town of Lineville, which was six miles away. For those of us from Barfield, Lineville was a booming metropolis – after all, it had one stop signal.

To me, Barfield was 'lily white'. The few Black families that lived there were controlled and spread out to the point that I only saw my friends on Sunday when we took the old mule-drawn wagon to church. I remember having to travel a long way by foot through heavily wooded areas just to play with my cousins. I tiptoed around the snakes and other wild creatures just to get to my cousins so I wouldn't be totally isolated.

Still, most of the time I had to make do playing alone, or with my sisters. Because when we moved to Barfield, it was for one purpose and one purpose only – to sharecrop.

With each passing year there came a different set of challenges, always something to do with racism and segregation. Our family struggled to make ends meet. There were, however, a couple of bright spots during our time in Barfield. Ma surprised us with a baby brother named Jerome. I was ten at the time and thought to myself, *you are one lucky little boy. You missed the adventures of sharecropping.* But Ma didn't stop there. She went on to surprise us again with a baby brother named Ronnie in January of 1957.

What was most interesting to me about our family was that we were all so different. My sister, Virginia, had an imagination that knew no boundaries. Ma used to say her imagination was enough to capture anyone's attention, and it did. It captured the imagination of all us siblings. We made a point of watching Virginia as she observed various animals. She could observe animals and birds for hours.

Virginia loved watching birds build their nests and feed their young. So, this one morning we spotted her sitting motionless. This went on for more than an hour. I suppose it could've gone on longer if the Hummingbird hadn't finished pollinating the flowers and left.

Virginia did this day after day, until this one day when we went to check on her, we discovered that she was up on the top of the barn with a corn shuck in each hand. Before we could stop her, Virginia jumped off the barn roof flapping her arms, and holding on to the corn husk. Why the corn husk? We never found out. But what was obvious to the rest of us was that Virginia had convinced herself from watching that Hummingbird that she could fly!

Being the oldest, Virginia had more chores than the rest of us. She picked cotton until around 11 am every day. Then she would go back to our shack and fix our dinner (which is what we called lunch). After dinner, she would return to the field and pick more cotton until about half an hour before sunset. Then she would return to the family shack and prepared supper. She never complained. Virginia was an average cotton picker, even though she would have much preferred to observe animal life instead. My sister, Barbara, was a great cotton picker. Fact is, she was good at whatever she put her mind to. Yes, sir. Once Barbara set her mind on a task, she would see it through. Her only issue was that she got picked on by others because she had that 'good hair.' She had what people called 'Indian hair.' And because she was a 'high yellow' attractive girl, that combination caused her some grief among adults and her peers growing up.

My sister, Joyce, and I shared a close bond. We played a lot together. We'd spend our idle time playing hide and seek with our cousins until we were exhausted. Joyce was then, and still is, very talkative. She was always interested in what others were doing. She always wanted to know what your thoughts were. She didn't share her thoughts until she knew what yours were. She was two years younger than me. She wasn't much of a cotton picker — I'll never forget the first morning I went to the cotton field fully prepared to pick cotton. I had just turned five and was still small in stature. But as far as my father was concerned, I was big enough for him to hang a small cotton sack across my shoulders.

That morning, as we were heading out to the field, the spectacle of all that cotton caught my attention. I said to Ma, "Look yonder, Ma. Look at all of that cotton."

Ma replied, "Well, I spec we'd better git out there and make that field dark like us. Because rat now, I feel like a speck of black pepper on an island of salt."

I didn't make much of it then, but as I matured, I realized that her comments were two-fold. She was referring to the neighborhood and to the cotton. At any rate, I miss all those funny little sayings Mama use to say.

Mama often reminded me that Barfield was the place where I first experienced what it was like to be a person of color. She told me way back then that my experiences there would go a long way toward shaping me into the person I am today.

Being the third child, and the first boy child to a family of sharecroppers in an area where other Black families were miles away, put a definite strain on my people skills. It was in Barfield I began to understand, firsthand, how Blacks were perceived by most whites.

Being treated differently because of the 'color of my skin and not the content of my character' marked the beginning of an important change in my development. It was a turning point because before then, Ma had taught me that if I treated people with respect, they would treat me with respect in return.

My first truly hurtful encounter with bigotry was at one of the town's General Stores where all of these old racist white men would assemble.

There were times when I went to the general store with my sisters. I was supposed to be their chaperon. But given how tough my oldest sister was, a chaperon for them I was not. But this was something that Ma wanted me to do.

Barfield was the proud possessor of three General Stores. This one store in particular always had what you wanted, but there was always a price to pay to get it. That store was the local hangout for old white bigots and rednecks.

My sisters hated going there and I found it very creepy myself. I was afraid, but I couldn't show it. These old white men,who had Blacks working for them, gathered at this store to exchange lies, play checkers, and harass Black customers. They loved to pick on my sisters and me. They all wanted to sniff at my sisters and my sisters wanted no part of it.

We weren't allowed to move around in the store and pick what we wanted to purchase. We had to wait by the register for the store owner to pull the items Ma had listed on a paper. We hated it. We had to stand right in front of those old white bigots and endure whatever insults came out of their mouths.

I remember this one time at the General Store when Homer, who had a nose that appeared to be twice the size of a normal nose, said to his friends, giggling, "I can't get over what a cute little Nigger boy he is. Come here, boy!"

So, when I stepped to him, he started rubbing my head. His friends asked him, "What in de hell is you doin', Homer?"

"Tain't nobody told you dat it's good luck to rub a Nigger's hair?"

"Why no. You sure 'bout dat? Because I don't want to be rubbing that wiry shit for nothin'!"

Old Homer replied, "Does a bear shit in the woods?"

Then came their loud uncontrollable laughter that bordered on hysteria. I knew all the while that I was powerless and incapable of any kind of a real reprisal. They had treated me this way so often, the effect it had on me was neutralized. It got to where, during those encounters, I would focus on one of Ma's sayings. One of the things she told me was, "Son, life builds character, experiences build wisdom."

I never was able to adjust to the anger I felt when they all took turns rubbing my head. That proved to be a scar that left its mark on me for most of my life. Rubbing my head and knocking me around like I was piñata left me with the understanding of what Dr. Martin Luther King, Jr. meant when he said, "We've got some difficult days ahead."

Days later, when Ma got word of what had happened at the General Store, she was as mad as spit on a griddle, "Them old snuff dipping, tobacco-chewing white men that hang around that store outta be shot. Shameless creeps! Pickin' on chil'ren jus' because they Black!"

Ma's comments made me wonder out loud about a lot of things that I didn't understand. Up until my tenth birthday, racial encounters, for the most part, always went from bad to worse. Then later, in the fifties, after I had grown a bit, my racial encounters went from worse to worse.

THE SHARECROPPER OWNER'S SON

I pointed out earlier how there were no Black kids nearby for me to play with in Barfield. Well, the same problem existed for the sharecropper owner's son. There were other white families in the area, but most of them were older and their kids were all grown up and living elsewhere.

A simple solution to this problem would be for our parents to let his son and me play together. So, sure enough, this one day the share crop overseer sent word to the cotton field for me to come to the Big House and play basketball with his son.

I was excited about that. It felt good to have a boy close to my age to play with! It was like a new beginning for me. I couldn't wait to match my ball skills against the ball skills of his kid. As I headed to the big house, there was a definite bounce in my step … until I met Mister Rat-Off.

(In movies that dealt with slavery, Mister Rat-Off was the man who rode the big white horse and watched over the slaves. Mister Rat-Off is a name that was more legend than something actually rooted and grounded in fact. Legend has it that this slave owner would say to his slaves, if he thought they were being idle, "If you don't get busy, I'll git rat off this hoss and git rat on yo' Black ass!")

As I was approaching the house, Mister Rat-Off met me out on the road in front of the house. He was an imposing, intimidating figure. He stood 6' 8" tall. This giant grabbed me by my throat. When he did, I could barely breathe. This big man stared into my eyes and yelled, "My son wins! You understand me, boy?" I was scared shit-less.

Between coughs and trying to catch my breath, I replied, "Yes, sir!"

When I saw his son stroke a long shot that hit nothing but the bottom of the net, I knew he was a player who had game. I thought to myself, "I don't know what you're worried about? I couldn't beat this big old, lanky boy with my best shots."

This boy was tall like his father. He stood about 6'6". And, believe it or not, he was just a couple of years older than me. We were both tall for our age. I stood six feet two inches in an era when tall was not in fashion. It was an era where other kids were cruel with their comments. I got tired of kids passing me in the hallway at school asking me, "How's the weather up there?"

Before we started the game, his father made sure I saw him sitting, watching from the window of the house. He wanted to make sure I didn't play my best, even though my best wouldn't have been good enough.

His son detected right away that I could play better and that I wasn't playing my best because of something his father had said to me. So, he confronted his father, "Why can't you just let us play, Dad? It doesn't matter who wins!" But his father was so blinded by bigoted hate, he couldn't see that my best effort against his son would not have been good enough. His son was clearly better at the game than I was. This would've been obvious to a blind man. But this bigoted man wasn't able to see that his son could handle his own with a basketball.

When his son slammed the ball down and ran off crying, I could see what could have been a positive thing slipping away.

The mother came out and took her husband to task, asking him about what he had done and telling him that he needed to stop the way he was handling things regarding his son. She looked at him and threw her hands up in disgust and headed over to me as I sat crying.

I don't know if I was crying for myself, or for his son. I did realize, however, that I'd rather be in the field picking cotton than sitting around and living in his situation.

The mother asked me if I would like to have lunch with her son. I replied, "Yes ma'am, I'd like that very much."

Those words were hardly out of her mouth when the father intervened and made his wife feed me on the back porch with the dogs. This, in spite of protests from her and her son. After being put on the back porch where I had to fight off flies, gnats, and dogs for my food, food that tasted good going down soon became like gravel in my gut. As I walked home, I was able to vomit most of it up.

There's no doubt, all that drama had to do with one man's racist beliefs. His actions were so disturbing, they made my walk home, under what was a punishing sun all the more painful.

I was hurt because I was a kid, and I enjoyed a competitive game. His restrictions didn't allow me to play my best. I cried all the way home. I truly believe that if this father hadn't been such an idiot and had promoted his son the right way, his son could have probably been another Jerry West, Magic Johnson, or Kobe Bryant. He was potentially that good.

I never played with him again. His son told me years later that, after that day, he never picked up a basketball again.

The year was 1950. I was to start school in a few months at the ripe old age of five. I could hardly contain my excitement. Then I realized I had no shoes to wear. So, I went to my mother who was getting her scalp scratched by my sister, Virginia. (Scratching the scalp was a ritual most southern women did before they washed their hair. The scratching loosened any dandruff.) I approached my mother and said, "Ma, school is starting soon, and I don't have any shoes to wear."

My mother looked at me through that long thick hair of hers. Then she looked down at the Bible that was laying across her lap. She began to weep. I went over to her, and she laid those big brown, wet eyes of hers on me and said, "Son, all of Mama's little credit accounts are at their limit. Ya Mama ain't got no idea what she's goin' to do rat now, but give Mama some time and she'll figure sumthin' out."

I felt bad for bothering my mother. I knew she was hell- bent on providing for her children. She made sure our needs were met. I don't know how she did it. There were mornings when she left for work singing an old Negro hymn, faced with the task of walking three miles to work and three miles home.

On most days when school was out and Ma couldn't ride the bus, she'd walk to work, earn less than $2.00 a day, and then walk home again. Sometimes a generous soul driving past Ma would stop and give her a lift.

Ma was faced with the demanding needs of her four children. Never once did she say, "Mama's tired. Go away!"

The weekend before the start of school, Ma decided to make a last-ditch effort at Elmer Cole's General Store to get her credit limit increased. She was hoping that Mr. Cole would be sympathetic and extend her a little more credit. On the way to the store, I was happy and playful. I had no idea that my need for shoes was bringing added pressure on my mother amidst a surging rat plague at our house. I had forgotten all about that problem.

On the way to the General Store, Ma was hopeful and said, "If anyone will give me credit, it'll be Mr. Cole. After all, I've cleaned his house, off and on, for more years than I care to remember."

We finally arrived at the store. Ma wasted no time in approaching Mr. Cole. She quietly asked him if he could give her just a little more credit. She explained her situation. Mr. Cole started whining and complaining so loudly that anyone in the store could hear him go on and on about how much Ma owed and why he couldn't extend her any more credit.

Mr. Cole created such a commotion that it drew the attention of an old fat, overall-wearing, snuff-dipping redneck. He started watching and listening to everything Mr. Cole said. So, when Ma started to walk out of the store, after being turned down by Mr. Cole, that old dirty, rotten scoundrel approached Ma with this devilish ear-to- ear grin on his face.

I didn't know what to think when he beckoned for Ma and they both moved away from me. But I did manage to hear him say, as Ma was walking away from him after their private conversation had dried up, "If'n you change your mind, gal, dem shoes is still on de table."

I had no idea he was attempting to trade shoes for sex; but for some reason, when Ma stormed out of that store, with tears swimming down her face, I knew then I didn't want those shoes. I caught up with her and said, "Ma, I can go to school barefooted."

Ma, turned and stared at me for a long time before saying, "Okay, son. And hopefully, we'll be lucky enough to have an Indian summer and it'll stay warm 'til late fall. By that time, Mama should be able to git you some shoes."

THE SOLUTION TO THE RAT PROBLEM

When we got back home from Elmer Cole's store, my mother was emotionally drained and needed to rest. But my unsympathetic father kept us all awake late that night shooting rats. This had become a regular routine for him on certain nights. My father shot those rats inside the house with a 22-caliber rifle, using a rat cartridge similar to the ones below. It was a rat shot that was perfect for a close-up situation where you need the effect of a shotgun- style pellet pattern with much less power.

I must admit it was clever how my father did it. He would sit by the bedroom door in his dirty wife-beater t-shirt and say to me when it was rat-killing time, "Jerry Donald, turn off all them lights in the hallway and turn on that spotlight in the kitchen and spread them crumbs on the floor under that light."

Then, sure enough, the rats would show. And when they did, he would sit there and pick them off one by one with that rifle. We all hated those rats, but my father especially hated them, and he had good reason to. (I will explain that later.)

I slept with my father because he suffered badly from PTSD (Post Traumatic Stress Disorder). It was unsafe for my mother, or anyone else, to sleep with him, but someone had to do it and I was elected.

There was a lack of space and a shortage of beds in our two-room, shot-gun-style shack with a small kitchen. In one of the rooms, there was a bed for my aunt who had had a failed marriage and moved in with my mother. There was a bed for my grandfather, and a big pallet-style bed for my aunt's daughter and my three sisters. In the room where I slept, there were two beds: one queen-sized bed for Mama and Jerome, and a double bed for my father and me.

Sleeping with my father was scary. Some nights it was touch and go. Like the night my father threw his arm across my neck, and it was so big and heavy I was unable to lift it off. I could barely breathe.

Incidences like that took place all too often. I felt hemmed in because I had to sleep on the side of the bed next to the wall. I remember this one night when my father was having a nightmare. He seemed to be fighting off the Japanese. He was screaming and kicking and yelling for his comrades. Then he grabbed me and pinned me against the wall so hard that it cracked the sheet-rock. Again, I couldn't breathe!

Luckily for me, Ma heard all the commotion and managed to get him awake and off of me. She was always there to bail me out of trouble during Daddy's restless PTSD nights.

My father hated those rats because this one night, I was awakened by this loud, irritating, crunching noise. My father was asleep and snoring loudly. I looked in the direction the sound was coming from, and I saw these beady eyes looking back at me. I blinked and they stayed right where they were. I was beyond scared. This was my worst nightmare.

I saw this huge rat gnawing on my father's foot! I screamed and kicked the covers off us. Ma quickly turned on the light, using the string that ran from the ceiling light to the bed frame. All the while, Daddy was still snoring. As I was getting up, the rat was on the floor by now, but was not rushing away in fear as rats normally did. No! This rat sat there and stared back at me before slowly crawling away, as if to say, "You're going to get your fill of messing with me when I'm eating."

Now, in fairness to that rat, my father's feet were grotesque. They had an ash tone to them that neither grease nor lotion could take away, not to mention their foul-smelling stench. When I complained to my mother about not being able to sleep with my father anymore because of how his feet smelled, and how loud he snored, she looked at me and shook her head, knowing that most of my fear was stemming from seeing that rat in the bed.

In her always-knowing-what-to-say-or-do manner, Ma began to explain to me what a brave hero my father was. She said, "Some of what's troublin' ya father has to do with them takin' him away from his home, such as it was, to go and fight for this country that thinks of him as somethin' lower than a pig."

Then Ma added, "And because of that stinkin' war, you've seen how there are nights when yo' daddy, through no will of his own, jumps out of bed screamin' 'Halt! Who goes there?!' Then there are nights when he becomes so frantic, he does all sorts of crazy things. After callin' out orders to his comrades in arms, he grabs that loaded shotgun and points it at you, then at me, and then all over the place."

"As to his feet, son, they are that way because he had to wear his boots (which were wet most of the time) for 22 days straight durin' some intense all-out fightin', without a chance to take 'em off."

Even though I was young at the time, I hung my head in shame. Ma knew it and said to me, "I'm proud of you, son, for bein' able to forget your own troubles in the face of what your father is dealin' with."

MOM AND DAD

My mother and father were different. They were not the usual run-of-the-mill parents. My father, Amos Boyd, was a big burly Black man with an angry stare. He had simple interests. He was a man of few words, never any lectures or lengthy reprimands. But the truth is, he was an angry man with many needs, and because of that, it was difficult to establish a close relationship with him as his son. Which forced me to live between two worlds: (1) striving to be perfect for him, and (2) trying to avoid his disapproval of me. I thank God that he wasn't mean and vindictive. Even though he had his challenges with life and was very angry about them, for the most part, he never took his troubles out on me, and I was never scared and anxious in his presence.

My father, Amos Boyd

Aware of my inquiring mind, Ma, felt the need to explain my father's behavior toward me. She would always start by saying, "Yo' father is a good man, son. He just go about doin' some things the wrong way. But there's no need to feel bad. Shucks, I remember when your father idolized Joe Louis so much that he lived vicariously through him, to the neglect of his family, including me. When Joe Louis lost to Max Schmeling, he actually sulked like a child and refused to work 'til Joe won later in a rematch."

That explanation was one that stayed with me. Years later, after the war, everything seemed to be 'hunky-dory again.' Sugar Ray Robinson had soared into prominence as the world's welterweight champion. By now, my sisters and I had become old enough to listen to the fights with my father. It was what was commonly referred to as "family night". Fact is, it was about all that we could do as a family and call it entertainment.

My mother, Eunice Dicy Boyd

On fight night, we would all gather around this old floor-model radio adorned with coat hangers- and foil to get the best noisy signal we could. The speakers were busted and that added to the distortion of good sound. We all sat close together and listened intensely. It took that kind of an effort to hear anything you could make sense of. I remember this one fight night Daddy was out of the room making snacks for the fights. Ma had us to herself and she talked to us about why she believed Daddy was so reliant on the outcome of those fights. She thought it was because of this deep-seated resentment he harbored against white people. She said because he knew that he couldn't express his anger and resentment of white people in real life, he did it through Black boxers.

She said, "In his mind, it is as close as he could come to beating white men—using the fists of those fighters." This helped me to understand my father's behavior when a Black fighter lost. He took it personally. When a Black boxer won, Daddy would walk around with his chest out, smiling and happy.

My mother, Eunice Dicy Boyd, was a very wise woman. I think of her often when I'm challenged to make a critical decision. There are times when it's like God is speaking to me in my mother's voice.

My memory of her is vivid. She was a good-looking, paper-sack-tan woman. She had a figure that gave rise to jealous women displaying upturned noses. She was a woman who didn't listen to outside noise; she was committed to her family and protected her children.

When Ma found out about Daddy's birdbrained scheme to keep us out of school to pick cotton, she said, "Amos! No!! Absolutely not! Them children are not goin' to wind up like me with no learnin'. Them children goin' to stay in school!"

SCHOOL DAYS

So off to school I went... barefooted. And sure enough, we had an Indian summer. Near the end of it, I got my new shoes. And during my first year of school, I received glowing support from my teacher. She told Ma that I was doing amazing work and that I would be a valedictorian candidate if I kept it up.

Second grade was something entirely different. Things happened that killed that desire in me to "Be the best of whatever I could be."

I didn't know it then, but I was subjected to some cruel and unusual responsibilities. Things that wound up causing me to lose my desires for school altogether.

At the outset of second grade, things began to go terribly wrong. I became aware that we were being bused past this well-kept school simply because we were Black. My spirit was crushed. Even more so when the bus rolled up in front of this old, broken-down, dilapidated building we were to be schooled in.

The very first day of class, it was evident to me that my second-grade teacher had singled me out. Even though I did not know why, it still felt good to be singled out. It felt like I had been accepted by her on merit.

SCHOOL DAYS 1956 - '57
Clay Co. Training

School photo of me in 1956

Then, near the end of the school day, as she leaned against the blackboard, she fixed her gaze on me. One that started to feel like an intimidating 'staredown' as she peered over her creepy-looking, wire-rimmed glasses and shouted, "You! Yes, you!"

Feeling privileged and pleased with the way things were going, I answered excitedly, "Yes, ma'am!"

And this is when things took a turn for the worst. She informed me that I was to be the class's HYGIENE INSPECTOR. I was delighted with her and myself, even though I had no idea what a Hygiene Inspector was. I began to understand exactly what it was I was supposed to do. The smile on my face froze as she continued to describe the gruesome duties of the Hygiene Inspector.

I was assigned to sniffing armpits, smelling breaths, and sniffing seats after someone farted.

Just moments before, I was beaming from ear-to-ear with a boyish smile. Then my insensitive teacher noted the change in my behavior and asked adamantly, "What's wrong with you, son?"

I responded with a whimper like that of a baby in need of sympathy. But when I saw her unveil this belt-like object that was taken from a horse's bridle and converted into a strap, I suspended all my personal feelings for fear of being punished with that strap.

Now, in fairness to the teacher, that room did stank to high heaven. It had a pissy, feces, armpit, bad breath kind of smell to it. That, she was not willing to forgive. This teacher believed that we could do better. She did not accept the age-old adage that this was one of the things that came with teaching second grade.

Talk about a dilemma. Going home and telling Ma I didn't want to be the Hygiene Inspector was tantamount to asking for a whipping, because Ma would automatically take sides with the teacher. So, with a whipping looming over my head at school, and another one when I got home, I had no choice.

I remember being so tormented at first. I decided that I wanted no part of third grade. No sir. I was content to go to the fields with my father rather than deal with things like that at the next grade level.

The chores of a Hygiene Inspector were nauseating and

disgusting, but thanks to God, none of it had a negative effect on me. In fact, as I grew older, I made jokes about it. I referred to myself as the ol' "seat sniffer."

When called upon, I would swing into action as my classmates watched in awe. I would put my ability to sniff, smell, and discern odors–and who did it–on full display.

FUGITIVE

T'was the night before Christmas in 1957. The night began innocently enough. Even though I no longer believed in Santa Claus, I went to bed early as my mother requested. Then, lo and behold, at 3 a.m. I suffered through a horrible nightmare that was so real I couldn't stop trembling. I had a physiological reaction, which required me going outside to do my business, because we had no indoor toilet.

Going to the outhouse by myself was no big deal normally, but that night before bed, my uncle had told a bunch of haunted house stories. Now, coupled with my nightmare, I was so fearful I couldn't muster up the courage to go out by myself.

I asked Ma to ask my father to go outside with me. When she did, they got into a heated argument. Ma was pleading with my father, "Amos, Jerry has had a terrible nightmare, probably because of Jim's stories and he's in shock. Can you go outdoors with him?"

My father retorted, "Shock, my ass! That boy can go out there by hisself!"

As I started to leave, fearful and despondent, my mother said, "Wait, son. I'll go with you"

My father yelled, "Like hell, you will! You need to stop babying that stupid ass boy!"

My mother then pleaded with him harder, "He adores you, Amos. And please don't talk so loud!"

My father shouted back, "You think I care what that fool boy hears!"

At this point, I tiptoed quietly closer to where they were. Ma, thinking that I was outside said, "He's not stupid! He's just searching for his identity. He loves you and tries to bond with you, but you are so blinded by hate you can't see it. He needs a father figure, Amos."

At this point, my father, the man I truly loved, went berserk. His comments sent a shock wave through my entire being. At the top of his voice, he screamed, "Then send him to Ohio where his old, stupid ass, slimeball father is!"

Realizing that the man I had been calling Daddy...wasn't daddy after all, time stood still. This was a moment that was truly timeless. To this day, that memory brings with it sadness.

I laid back down that night. I tossed and turned, unable to sleep. Time drew out as slow as molasses. Finally, as the sun cleared the horizon on Christmas morning, I got up without the usual excitement I always managed to have on Christmas morning.

With a need to be alone, I went to the edge of the woods. I always went there when I wanted solitude, and I needed solitude this Christmas morning. Everything had been turned upside down the night before.

So, when Ma called, I managed to make my way back to the house and to the gift-opening ritual where my little brother, Jerome, was enthusiastically opening his gifts under a strange-looking Christmas tree.

The tree was very tall and had a weird bend. The trunk

Childhood Christmas tree

was gnarled and mysterious-looking. At first, I tried to make it be a fir, then a spruce. Then, after remembering what they both looked like, neither one of them made sense. So, my conclusions were that it had to be a cedar in an ugly sort of way. Whatever it was, that thing went from the floor to the ceiling. And, as it pushed against the ceiling, it took on a hunchbacked appearance that made it look like it was about to greet you.

For something that was used to represent Jesus's birthday, one of the tree's branches looked like a witch's finger reaching for the heavens. At any rate, watching my little brother's enthusiasm didn't stop the sadness I felt. And it didn't help matters when I realized that me and my sisters only got a bag of apples and oranges.

I left the room crying, followed by my mother who said, "Son, Ma only had enough money to git a few things for your little brother. You know I only makeTa dollar and fifty cents a day and that doesn't go very far."

I said, "Ma, how can they expect you to walk three miles, work all day, then turn around and walk three miles home after work, and only pay you --"

"I'd walk twenty miles a day for less money if I had to, just to feed my family. Now Mama has some pennies and a silver dollar that she was tryin' to save, but you can have it."

"Ump! I wanted some new clothes, Ma! Can't nobody do nothing around here, but work!"

"Come on now, son. Don't mess up Christmas for your little brother. Be a big boy, okay?"

So, we returned to the tree room. Ma, in an effort to ease my pain, grabbed one of my little brother's gifts, "Look what your little brother got for Christmas." She handed me a small guitar and left the room to get dinner started.

I stroked it gently, but a string broke. Jerome saw what happened and began to scream.

My stepdad appeared out of thin air. "What did you do?" He saw the guitar. "You stupid idiot!"

"I... I... I didn't do nothing. I don't know. I.. just... it broke... and... aah it broke itself."

"You think I'm stupid?!"

"No, sir. I could never think of you like that. I wanted you to be my dad. I wanted that more than anything in the world."

"Well, I'm not, you stupid-looking piece of shit!" "Please! Give me a chance. I promise to be the best son you could ever have."

And that's when he struck me violently, knocking me across the bed and against the wall, causing me to fall underneath the bed. Screaming to me under the bed, my stepfather yelled, "You bastard! You didn't have no business touching his things!"

At this point, my mother entered the room and screamed, "You leave that boy alone! I mean it, Amos!"

While they were arguing, I snuck out from under the bed and quietly left home. I made my way to the woods. I sat down and leaned against a pine tree. After a while, I fell asleep. I was awakened by the sound of a gunshot. A hunter was shooting at a rabbit and the rabbit was close by me!

I sat there until it was close to sunset before making my way to the road. I knew the area pretty well and understood how to hitchhike, because I had started hitchhiking on this same road to go get my haircut over in Hopson City. I had only done that about three times but still made the decision that this route was best for me.

The first car to stop was a station wagon with wood panels. We used to call these a 'woody'. The man rolled down his window and I recognized him as one of the white men at the General Store— one of the men who was always gazing and staring at my sisters when they came in there to shop.

"Where you goin', boy?" "Ohio."

"Well...I'm going as far as North Carolina."

Not knowing North Carolina was about 700 miles away, I just hopped in. I was glad to get a ride.

I sat quietly in his station wagon as he drove down the road. Things began to feel uncomfortable. He looked over at me strangely.

"You runnin' away, ain't you, boy?" "Yes, sir."

"Do you know what you're runnin' to?" I never will forget those words.

I began stumbling over my words. I didn't know what to say.

"You scared shitless, ain't you, boy?" "Yes sir,"

"Why don't you go back home?"

I heehawed, mumbled, and stumbled over my words. I was scared. I finally blurted out, "I can't."

The man continued driving in silence. I believe he was assessing the situation. Then he said, "The way I see it, your Daddy gave you a beatin', didn't he, boy?"

I thought to myself, *He knew!*

While he continued to drive, he tried to convince me to go back home. I began to trust him. It was dark by now. He turned off the main road and headed down a small dirt road.

"I gotta make a quick stop. Then we'll be headed on out."

He came upon an old racing facility. It was dark and scary. He pulled up to this old building and stopped. As we sat there, a huge tree branch fell and hit the hood of his station wagon. It rolled off. The man didn't move; he didn't budge. I should have known something was wrong. It got very quiet.

I sat and stared into the night. I tried to see something outside – anything. I looked all around. It was pitch black. I couldn't see anything. When I turned back, the man had opened the glove compartment. He took a pistol out. It was big and shiny in the dark. No words were exchanged. My heart began to beat fast. He put the pistol on the dashboard.

Then he laid his hand on my leg. I didn't know what that meant. He kept it there for a moment. Then he moved his hand closer to my crotch. At twelve, I knew this was wrong. I was scared. I moved away. He started snatching at my zipper. He couldn't get it opened. He violently ripped it open! I was in shock. He proceeded to molest me. No words were spoken.

As he was molesting me all sorts of thoughts crossed my mind. I remember Ma telling me that Jews were God's 'chosen' people. That's why their churches and schools were better than ours. This man was white, so I thought he must be a Jew. As tears ran down my cheeks, I thought, God let me down. I used to want to be 'chosen' like them, but not now. If these are God's 'chosen' people, I don't want to be 'chosen.' I don't want to go to heaven anymore. After he molested me, he dragged me out of the station wagon and dumped me in the woods. He drove off. I sat alone and afraid in the dark. I heard all sorts of animal sounds. I got up and began walking to the road. I knew I was near Hopson City.

I walked along the road. Eventually, a car passed me. The car stopped and back up to where I was. The window rolled down. A middle-aged white man looked at me with concern.

"You okay, boy?" "Yes, sir."

"Where you goin'?" "I'm okay, sir."

"Where you goin', boy?" "Ohio."

"Ohio?"

I told the man what had happened to me. The man cursed that man for abusing me. He said, "I'm goin' to Atlanta...Georgia. Hop in."

I trusted him. I hopped in. I had no choice.

As we drove to Atlanta, this man asked me a lot of questions. I began to feel more comfortable. When we got to Atlanta, in the early morning, he took me to a Greyhound Bus Station and bought me a ticket to Dayton, Ohio. He said his good-bye and left. To this day, I call him my angel. When I looked at my ticket, I realized the bus to Dayton didn't leave until later that evening. So, I decided to walk around.

I met a group of three Black guys. They were all grown men – in their twenties. They asked me what I was doing. I told them I was waiting for the bus to Ohio, but it didn't leave until that evening. They invited me to a party. I went with them, but I was so tired when we got to the party, I sat down and fell asleep between two speakers. Bobby Blue Bland's "Further On Up the Road" was blaring. I was awakened by a fat, greasy Black man who had my hands cupped in his over his nipples squeezing them! He leaned over and tried to kiss me. I panicked. I felt that he was going to take advantage of me and try to molest me. I couldn't let that happen. I had to get away.

"Let me go to the bathroom first."

I got up and headed to the door. He said, "Where you goin'?"

"To pee!"

"The bathroom's over there."

"In the house?" I had never seen an indoor toilet. I couldn't believe it.

Then he got up and led me to the indoor bathroom. On the way, I saw men hugging, kissing, and fondling one another. I had never seen that before. My world was turning upside down. Once inside this bathroom, I sat on the commode pondering my situation. I happened to look behind me and I noticed the window was opened.

Then someone tried to open the door. The handle was rattling! I panicked. I climbed up on the windowsill and jumped out the window. The area outside the window was dark, but I jumped anyway. It had to be a ten to twelve- foot drop. I landed in an ocean of shit! There were piles and piles of feces floating in gallons of urine under the window. The stench was awful.

I got up and walked down the road for about a mile, finally finding a service station on the outskirts of town. As I approached, a little old Black man saw me and came out of the station. He helped hose me off with water and gave me clean clothes (an old mechanic uniform). I told him my situation.

"If you head off down that stretch of road, you'll be fine. Just be careful. The first fifteen miles is an 'all white' stretch. Be careful. Ain't nothing but Crackers on that piece of road."

Before I had walked a mile down that road, a Camaro filled with a carload of white teens passed me. It stopped and backed back. I could tell they had been drinking. They were yelling and laughing. Someone threw something wet on me. I don't think it was a watermelon because they weren't ripe yet. Whatever it was, it was soaked in liquid. It hit me in the face. I was blinded. They drove off, but then I heard someone yell, "Turn around!"

I heard the Camaro turn around. Good thing the blindness was temporary. I saw some teens jump out the Camaro. I started running as fast as I could. They chased me a good while. They couldn't catch me. I jumped over a fence and ran into the woods.

When I decided to come out of the woods, I noticed there was a little store with boxes out front. As a Greyhound Bus slowly pulled to a stop in front of the store, a Caucasian driver hopped out and began loading the boxes onto the bus. I went over and began helping him load the boxes. I told him about my situation – how I had lost my ticket, what had happened to me, and how badly I needed to get to Ohio.

He looked me straight in my face and said, "I can't help you if you don't have a ticket."

The driver got back on the bus and started to pull off. The bus stopped. The driver got out. He yelled back at me, "Come on, boy!"

I got on board. The bus was almost empty. "All the way to the back, boy!"

"Yes, sir."

The bus took me to Harrisburg, Pennsylvania. From Harrisburg, I eventually wound up in Dayton, Ohio. I had an address and, eventually, somebody showed me where my aunt's house was.

I knocked on her door. I was tired, dirty, filthy, nervous, traumatized. The door opened. My aunt looked at me and frowned.

"Where's yo' Mama?"

I explained that I had decided to live with my real father. She had me come inside. She made some calls. My father eventually came. As soon as I met him, I knew he didn't want me. I didn't want to go with him, but I did. I went to live with my real father and his wife. My father was cold and distant. We had no bond at all.

His wife, my new stepmother, didn't want me either. She began to lock up the food. One night I was so hungry, I decided to get a screwdriver and remove the refrigerator door. I laid the door on the kitchen floor and made me some eggs, ham, and toast. I knew I was in trouble. I remembered my stepmother kept a jar of dimes in the kitchen cabinet. I took the jar of dimes (about $15-$20 worth) and left. There was no coming back.

I was homeless. I was too ashamed to go home. I contemplated suicide several times. Whenever I considered jumping off a bridge, I could always hear Ma's voice, "Son, when the going gets tough, the tough get goin'."

Life on the street was rough. Some days I did not eat. Nights were scary and cold. I wandered around during the night to keep safe. I slept during the day. I hunted for food anywhere I could. One day, after struggling to find food and dealing with crazy people, I wrote Ma a letter. "Ma, I guess I'm not very tough." Then I called my school in Barfield and told a teacher there to contact my mother. She did.

One day, Ma came to the school and called me on a number I left. We talked over the phone. "Come home, son, your father didn't mean those words he said. We all miss you. Please come home."

Since I was tall for my age, I got a job washing cars. As soon as I saved up enough money to buy a bus ticket, I returned home.

It felt good to be back in Barfield, the only home I really knew. I missed my family. I needed my family. No matter the ups and downs in any family, there's still no place like home.

LOOKING BACK...

I've learned that forgiveness is the key to your mental and physical health. The Bible teaches us that we are to forgive others because we have been forgiven. Though difficult in the natural and seemingly hopeless at times, my ability to forgive was made easier when I attempted to stand in the other person's shoes. I had to understand the problems my stepfather and my biological father had to experience during that time in our history. Life had to be difficult for a Black man during the 40s and 50s in America when life was a struggle and racism was rampant.

Then, I took a giant step forward when I realized that hating someone who had made their transition was fruitless. I thank God every day that I got it fixed before resentment could cause disease and sickness to attach themselves to my body. I forgive both my fathers. I loved them both. May they rest in peace.

About the Author: Jerry Boyd
Actor / Author / Playwright / Minister

Jerry Boyd has been a member of the Screen Actors Guild and the American Federation of Television and Radio Artists since 1970. Most of his professional work has been on television.

Jerry enjoyed a recurring role on the hit television series *Hawaii 5-0*.

Mr. Boyd served his country for two tours overseas. After serving in the Philippines, he was transferred to Pearl Harbor, Hawaii. While stationed there, he decided he would audition for a role on *Hawaii 5-0*. He was cast as a pimp in an episode starring Glynn Turman. The acting bug bit and Jerry decided to leave the military after eleven years and pursue his acting dream. While in Hawaii, he was privileged to spend time with the renowned producer, Steven Bochco. Since that time, he has continued with his acting career as well as writing plays projects.

Jerry took inventory of his life and decided to leave the world of "skirts and drugs" and learn more about the Lord. Once he was back stateside, he joined Crenshaw Christian Center. A few weeks later, he decided to enroll in their School of Ministry. Since then, Jerry has devoted much of his time to ministering battered women and participating in the church's daily telephone intercession prayer line.

Mr. Boyd has been able to pursue his artistic side as well as his spiritual side. He says the combination works well for him.

TWO

WAITING FOR SOMEDAY

Patricia Forté

1945

PORT CHICAGO NAVAL MAGAZINE

Port Chicago was a small town on the southern banks of Suisun Bay in Contra Costa County in Northern California. It was located about a mile from the U.S. Navy munitions depot known as the Port Chicago Naval Magazine. (A magazine is a storage facility for explosives.) Ammunition storage and construction of Navy barracks in Port Chicago began shortly after the attack on Pearl Harbor, December 7, 1941.

The munitions stored at the Port Chicago depot included bombs, shells, naval mines, torpedoes, and small arms ammunitions–all destined for the Pacific Theatre. ('Theatre' indicated the region for military operations.) This new facility was ideal for munition transfer and loading. Since they were short on stevedores, Navy personnel had to perform loading duties.

From the beginning, all of the enlisted men employed as loaders were African American. All of the commanding officers were white. The enlisted men were trained for military duty but instead were put to work as stevedores. (Stevedores are longshoremen or dock workers.) None of these enlisted men had been trained in ammunition loading. None of the white officers had been trained in supervising ammunition loading.

Captain Merrill Kinne was named commander of the Port Chicago facility. He had come out of retirement in 1941. (He had served the Navy from 1915 -1922.) He had no training in loading munitions and very little experience in handling them.

Captain Kinne pushed the enlisted men to load explosive cargo as fast as they could – the goal was 10 tons per hatch per hour. Most loading officers considered this goal too high. Captain Kinne tallied each crew's average tonnage per hour on a large chalkboard. Junior officers placed bets with each other and coaxed their crews to load more than the others.

The enlisted men were aware of the illegal betting and were instructed to slow down when senior officers came around.

There was no system in place to make sure the officers and the enlisted men were familiar with safety regulations. The International Longshore and Warehouse Union offered to train the men but the Navy declined the offer.

THE GREAT EXPLOSION

On the evening of July 17, 1944, disaster struck. There was a great explosion in Port Chicago. The munitions detonated while being loaded onto a cargo vessel bound to cross the Pacific Ocean. The powerful explosion detonated in a fireball seen for miles. An Army Air Force pilot flying in the area reported the fireball being three miles in diameter. One ship was completely destroyed, another was blown out of the water and torn into sections. A Coast Guard fireboat was thrown 600 feet upriver. Barracks and other buildings were severely damaged.

There was nearly $9.9 million in damages. ($145 million in 2020.) The seismograph at the University of California, Berkeley, measured the larger shock wave to be 3.4 on the Richter Magnitude Scale.

All 320 men on duty at the pier died instantly. Of the 320 dead, only 51 could be identified. 390 civilians and military personnel were injured, many seriously.

African Americans' injuries totaled 202 dead and 233 injured, which accounted for 15% of all African American casualties during World War II.

BOARD OF INQUIRY

A Naval Board of Inquiry was held on July 21, 1944, to find out what happened. The proceedings lasted 39 days. Captain Kinne's posted tonnage competition came to light. The Navy determined that the tonnage competition was not at fault. No officers were found guilty of wrongdoing. The report stated that the cause of the explosion could not be determined, but it implied that mistakes by the enlisted men were the main reasons. There was no mention of the enlisted men's lack of training.

The Navy asked Congress to give each victim's family $5,000. Representative John Rankin (D-Miss) insisted the amount be reduced to $2,000 when he learned most of the dead were Black men. Congress settled on $3,000. Years later, on March 4, 1949, heirs to 18 merchant seamen killed in the explosion were granted a total of $350,000. (That's $19,000 plus per family!)

For Black enlisted men, World War II was a war against fascism on foreign soil, but also a war against racism at home.

SURVIVORS

The surviving men who helped put out the fires and saw the horrors firsthand were quickly reassigned to Mare Island Naval Shipyard. (This shipyard was the first U.S. Navy base established on the Pacific Ocean. It was located 25 miles from San Francisco.)

Less than a month later, when ordered to load more munitions but still having received no training, 258 African American sailors refused to carry out the order. Two hundred and eight were charged with bad conduct and had to pay forfeitures. The remaining fifty men were put on trial for a general court-martial. They were sentenced to between 8-15 years hard labor.

In 1999, President Bill Clinton granted a pardon to Freddie Meeks, one of the few sailors still alive. Two years later, they were all given clemency. A 1944 review of the trials revealed race played a large part in the harsh sentences.

In 2019, a resolution was introduced in the 116th United States Congress. It recognized the victims in the explosion and officially exonerated the fifty men court-martialed by the Navy.

This horrific event highlighted systemic racial inequality in the Navy.

This was the atmosphere awaiting my father when he decided to come to California in the '40s to find work. In 1944, Daddy worked as a stevedore in Port Arthur, Texas. I understand Daddy had to leave in a hurry because he had whipped some white man's ass who had disrespected him. He happened to see a flyer that said Port Chicago, in California, needed dock workers. Since he was a stevedore, he jumped at the opportunity.

Moving West

"Blanche, I'm gonna take 'em up on this offer. They need dock workers real bad out there in Port Chicago. I got to borrow some money and get the car ready for the road. Pack me some clothes."

Mama studied the flyer on the table; the flyer that would change our lives.

"Okay, Odell. If you think this is a good move. I'll make you a big lunch for the road. I'll fry you a chicken, with some potato salad and light bread. (Light bread was Wonder bread.) Keep the salad in the ice bucket. You be careful out there on the road by yourself. Find yourself a safe place to sleep. We're gonna miss you."

Without much fanfare, Daddy got the car ready for the journey. Mama packed his lunch, and soon he was gone—rolling down the highway on Route 66.

We lived in the small farming town of Henderson, Texas, at the time. We lived on the family homestead there. The discovery of oil in Henderson in 1930 created a booming economy in the area. The population went from 2,000 to 10,000 in a few months. The oil fields in and surrounding Henderson provided a large part of the town's economy.

Mama had her hands full watching five energetic kids by herself. (My younger brother, Glenn, was born in California.) Daddy was gone for a few weeks. Once Daddy found work in Port Chicago as a stevedore, he drove back to Texas to get his family and start his new life.

My parents were always concerned about the safety of their

boys growing up in the South. The South did not tolerate any misbehavior from Negroes. Their boys' safety became more of an issue, the older they became. When we left Texas, Bo was 13, Alfred was 9, the twins were 5, and I was thirteen months.

Mama was excited about leaving Texas. She packed and talked. "I'm worried for my boys, Odell. Good thing we're moving out west. Here in the South, they don't stand a chance. I've seen too much. Heard the Klan is acting up again. There was a cross burning in Reverend Jenkins' yard last month."

Mama stuffed bags and boxes as she packed for her new life. "I saw a lynching when I was a little girl. Never will forget that sight. I don't want to ever see that again. My boys got to get outta here. I've heard about Negroes being castrated and burned. Remember that sailor they found a while back?"

Daddy listened; Mama talked. "Bo and Alfred are pretty much obedient boys. But those twins... Lord, I'm worried for 'em. Even at their young age, they're as wild as can be. They stay in trouble. It's just a matter of time before they upset some ol' white man. I've seen what these Crackers do to adventurous young Negro boys."

Being adventurous and curious was a bad combination for any Negro boys in the south in the 40s. My parents lived with the fear that one day one of their boys might cause the ire of some white bigot and wind up swinging at the end of a rope on some tree. That was not uncommon back then. (And that was before the world saw the horrific aftermath of white bigotry in the death of teenager Emmett Till in the 1950s. Mama made sure her boys saw the photo when it appeared in Jet magazine.)

Our family packed up our meager belongings and headed out West. We left the South like so many Black families did in the 1940s. We, too, were looking for a better life, a brighter future. We, too, were a part of that great migration that Isabella Wilkerson so eloquently captured in her book, *The Warmth of Other Suns*.

LIFE IN PORT CHICAGO

In the 1940s, Port Chicago was a small Navy town in

Northern California. That's where we lived when our family moved out West. The town has since been razed – leveled to the ground. We lived in an enclave of Port Chicago called Knox Park. The employees who worked at the naval shipyard all lived in Knox Park. Knox Park was also the name of the street that divided the small town. White families lived on one side and Black families lived on the other—and never the two should meet.

We kids were instructed early on to never, ever cross over to the other side. Racial tension was alive and well in Port Chicago. Mama and Daddy did not talk to us kids much about the racial situation. We just knew we had to be careful. We thought we had left racial strife in Henderson, but it was patiently waiting on us in Port Chicago.

Our family of eight lived in a small, two-bedroom unit alongside other employee units. Our unit was 51 Knox Park.

The one good thing about our unit was that it was at the end of a row of units. Our unit was next to the street. It had a huge Oak tree adjacent to the street. The neighborhood kids would come and play hide and seek with us well into the night.

In the 1940s there were no problems with kids playing outside until 8 or 9 o'clock, running, riding bikes, skating, pulling wagons, playing catch, stealing apples and plums from neighbors' back yards.

The town of Port Chicago had one school, Bay Point, that went from kindergarten to senior high. It was a newly built school. It was beautiful. I suspect they would have built another school for us Black kids, but they didn't

Me and my brother, Glenn, with my friends, Ethel Joyce and Tuna Fish

have the resources. We were usually the only Black student in the class. Sometimes, I got teased by the white kids because my hair was different. I loved learning so I could tolerate that.

The town had one very small circular library. It housed about 200 books. It had a small downtown district with one large grocery store. Then, there was the Chicken Shack at the edge of town for Negroes. That's where Negroes could eat fried chicken and pickled pig feet, drink some cold beer, talk a lot of crap, and dance to the sounds of B.B. King, Lowell Fulson, and T. Bone Walker.

We kids adjusted quickly to life in Port Chicago. We made friends and played. Daddy worked and came home in the evenings. Mama washed, cleaned, cooked, and worked in our garden. That was life as I saw it.

LIFE WITH FATHER

"Come here, gal!" "Yes, Mama."

"Where have you been?"

I don't know what to say. Whatever I say gonna get me in trouble. It's best I hold my head down.

"Cat got your tongue?"

"Mama, why can't I go across the street?"

"Because I said so, first of all. And because it's dangerous! You know you're not allowed to go over there." "That's not fair, Mama!" I held my head up, looking

Mama squarely in her eyes.

"Life is not fair! Now, where have you been? You think I'm crazy?! You've been gone for almost two hours. Nobody could find you."

"Mama, Jimmy said I could play with his big clown doll anytime I wanted. It's really something. It's the same size we are. You can hit it to the ground and it bounces right back! Wow! I think it's magic."

Mama could see the wonder in my eyes, but she knew the climate of the time.

"You cross that street at the wrong time and some Cracker see you, ain't no telling what he might do. You just can't trust everybody, Eileen. You stay on this side of the street. You hear me?"

"Yes, Mama."

"I don't want to have to tell your Daddy."

You never wanted Mama to tell Daddy about any misbehavior. That was sure death. Daddy always came home in a funk, and if Mama told him to discipline one of us, it seemed he took all his anger out on us poor kids. A whipping with a switch was always painful. We'd have to go and find our own torture tool! We'd go find a decent- sized branch with leaves and then remove the leaves before we gave it to him. No matter what bush you picked your switch from, the whipping was always so painful, especially if the whipping came from a miserable, devalued Black man.

"Mama, please don't tell Daddy! Pleeease! I won't do it again." I must have sounded like a broken record. "I won't do it again" was my mantra at the age of seven.

The men in our segregated community mostly worked at the Naval shipyard doing some type of menial labor. My father, Edgar Odell Berry, was not an enlisted man. He worked on the ships moving missiles, but I didn't know that then. All I remember is Daddy going to work and coming home distant and silent.

I didn't know that Daddy was working at a job that did not respect him, a job that made him feel inferior and subservient. I had no idea Daddy went to work every day to a job that stripped him of what vestiges of manhood he had. I couldn't understand why he was so sullen. Mama couldn't either.

"How'd it go today, Odell?" Mama tried her best to get some conversation out of Daddy. His response ranged from a low moan to, "It was alright."

Daddy was never one for small talk, we were told. We never knew what insults he must have experienced during his shift at the Naval base. Daddy was always so silent.

"I'm gonna make you some nice meatloaf sandwiches for your lunch tomorrow. I made an extra-large meatloaf for dinner tonight. I know you like spam, so I'm gonna make you some spam sandwiches for Friday." Daddy's response would be some guttural sound as he left the table. Mama was left to herself even though Daddy was only a few feet away. Each in their own world.

My father must have felt trapped like so many Black men in the 1940s and 50s. He was beholden to the white man for work to feed his family, but he hated him for stripping him of the right to decide his future. This country was recovering from Jim Crow restrictions and many folks refused to let it go.

DOMESTIC VIOLENCE

My mother was an educated woman who found herself burdened with eight children and a distant husband. She had some college, but I don't know how much. My sister, Ali Christine, died before I was born and my brother, Ronald Wayne, died of leukemia when I was very young.

In fact, we kids were in Carlsbad, New Mexico, with our grandmother when we got the news from Mama that Ronald had died. Mama had sent us there while she figured out a way to leave my father. In those days, women didn't have shelters for battered women. Women had to figure out, on their own, how to stay alive and raise their kids alone.

As far back as I could remember, my father had this bad habit of becoming MIA on the weekends. The men all got paid on Friday. The eagle flew every Friday back in those days. (The eagle referred to the eagle that appeared on the one-dollar bill.)

Daddy would get paid, come home, get dressed 'sharp as a tack,' and just leave. Yes. Daddy just left. Sometimes we kids would ask, "Where you goin', Daddy?" He usually responded with laughter as he headed for the door, "Oh, I'm going out with the dry cattle."

We never understood what that meant, but it somehow justified his departure. Mama never said anything. She kept her feelings to herself.

Daddy would be gone all weekend and come Sunday night to face Mama and us kids.

Daddy always looked spent – exhausted, drained, tired. He would sit at the kitchen table and sip on his favorite liquor, Old Crow. Old Crow was a low-priced brand of Kentucky-made straight bourbon whisky. Sometimes guilt propelled him into action.

Daddy would sit at the table and begin by cursing under his breath. That was the prelude. "Damn it to hell... Why in the hell...I'll be damned if I let that bastard..." We could never hear his total disgust with the world, but we knew he was unhappy. Then he would slowly raise his voice. Daddy was always soft-spoken and somewhat pensive; so, for him to raise his voice, you knew it was Old Crow talking. We kids sat in fear, knowing how this story would end.

Daddy would give Mama what money he had left. Mama seldom argued, but when she reached her limit, she and Daddy argued.

"Odell, how can I buy groceries with this? How can I pay the bills!"

My father mostly spoke under his breath, but we kids knew he was getting frustrated.

The horror of seeing my mother and father argue had psychological effects on all of us kids. Seeing my father hit my mother and knock her to the floor is a nightmare for any child. Daddy would hit Mama like she was a man. That was devastating to us kids. We screamed, we cried, we tried to help Mama. It was like seeing two gods fight one another. Our worlds were shaken. We loved them both; they were our gods.

"Stop! No, Daddy! Please don't!" If we got in the way, Daddy pushed us away. "Please, Daddy, stop!"

"Please don't hit Mama!" We all cried and screamed, but it meant nothing to my father. We tried to shield Mama. My younger brother and I could get away with more interference. My older brothers could not. Any move to help Mama on their part was seen as an act of defiance.

"Odell, stop! Please!" Mama's cries went unheeded as we sat on the sidelines crying and yelling for him to stop.

Two things happened as a result of Daddy's abuse. One thing that tore our family apart was the fact that my older brother, Bo, was forced to leave home because he and my father could not tolerate one another. As a young man, my brother felt obligated to protect his mother. Daddy kicked him out of the house when he was sixteen or seventeen. That broke Mama's heart. Bo was quiet and reserved and he and Mama were really close. Mama and Bo stayed in contact with one another, but their lives would never be the same.

The other thing that happened because of Daddy's abuse was that my brother, Odell, and I developed a speech disorder. Odell was a twin; he was named after my father. His twin's name was Donell. Odell's stuttering was more severe than mine. That disorder persisted throughout our childhood.

Funny thing about stutterers. They may stutter while speaking, but they can sing flawlessly. Odell eventually went into the armed forces. While stationed in Seoul, Korea, he sang in a Korean nightclub. They had articles about this American soldier singing in Korean in the newspaper there.

I had a stuttering problem during my early adolescent years. I believe I cured myself by avoiding certain sounds and letters. I had difficulty with words that began with "K," or "T", or the hard "C." I learned to replace certain words in my sentences so I wouldn't get stressed and stutter.

Both Odell and I have overcome this speech disorder. Every now and then, you'll hear it in his speech. But, for the most part, he is doing very well.

To this day, I am uncomfortable around a man who speaks too loudly. It brings back memories. I could never tolerate a man who yells at me or who abuses me physically. I have my dear Mama to thank for that.

On a few occasions, after Daddy would come home Sunday night in a stupor, and flop down to sleep, Mama would rouse us kids out of sleep late at night and quietly usher us out into the night. We knew the drill. Mama would quietly pack our clothes in bags and put us in someone's car. We'd ride in the night until she found us shelter. Mama was trying to figure out her life.

Back in the 1940s and 50s, women had to stay and tolerate abusive marriages. They had no refuge and no birth control, other than abortion. Mama found people who would keep us for a while. Sometimes she found friends, sometimes we stayed with her mother, Lila.

We'd stay away from Daddy for four or five weeks. By that time, he would have sweet-talked her into returning or Mama realized she was wearing out her welcome and decided to return to the only world available to her. She knew she had no other options.

MAMA'S STORY

Blanche Berry was a strikingly beautiful woman. She stood 5'2", with great facial features. She reminded me of the

Italian actress, Gina Lollobrigida, who was a popular actress in the 50s and 60s. Mama had fair skin and could have 'passed' for Spanish or Italian, but she refused. Some of our distant relatives 'passed' for white. I understand they

Mother, Blanche Berry – circa 1995

lived in fear that one day they could be betrayed by an offspring that did not look white.

Mama was not raised by her mother. She was raised by her mother's father, a Methodist pastor. I suspect it was because Mama had to be mixed with white blood. I don't know the circumstances of Mama's birth – whether she was the product of her mother's relationship with a white man or whether her mother was raped.

Mama sometimes talked about her early years. "Life with my grandfather was horrible. He was strict. He was distant. The only friend I had was my step-grandmother. She was kind to me. My grandfather was a Methodist pastor and he didn't tolerate much of anything. I had to be in church most nights. I did my homework there while my grandfather held meetings. The Wednesday night business meetings were scary. All the men, including my grandfather, carried guns to the meeting. He had a temper, and you never knew how the meeting would end. I would sit in the back pew hoping no one lost their temper."

"One day, my step-grandmother came to me. She looked sad. She said, 'Blanche, you know I love you, but I can't stay here any longer. If you were mine, I'd take you with me. I can't live in this hell any longer. Take care of yourself, baby. I love you.'"

Mama spent her adolescence living in a household with a distant, Methodist pastor. She and her mother became closer once she reached adulthood. All the while, her mother was raising another daughter, Aunt Margaret. These two sisters never met one another growing up.

I must have been around ten years old when I first met my Aunt Margaret. I do remember two things about my Aunt Margaret. I liked her as soon as I met her. She had the best set of teeth I'd ever seen. Her smile against her smooth chocolate skin was captivating. And I loved that mischievous look in her eyes. She was a plump woman in her thirties when I first met her. She was fun to be around. She knew how to talk to kids to make them feel comfortable. Aunt Margaret actually talked to us kids. She did not dismiss us as most adults did.

The other thing about Aunt Margaret bothered me. I sometimes overheard conversations between Aunt Margaret and my grandmother.

"Seems like to me, you treat Blanche like she was the Queen of Sheba. You go out of your way to do for her."

"Look, Margaret, Blanche is strapped with all these kids. Odell ain't got time for her or the kids. She needs our help."

"She needs to handle her own business."

"You know Odell ain't never home on the weekends.
She's all alone."

"I know, but still..."

"You know for yourself, he don't hardly give her any money to run the household."

"I know, I know, but she has to take care of that. That's

not our problem. You baby her too much, Mama. Blanche needs to stand on her own two feet. Whatever she needs, you try your damndest to give it to her."

Aunt Margaret always felt that my grandmother treated my mother better than her. These two sisters never did create a bond as adults.

PICKING COTTON

On those rare occasions when Daddy did stay home for the weekend, it was to go pick cotton to supplement our income. Our family drove to Dos Palos in the wee hours of Saturday morning. Dos Palos was a small ranching town. It had farms and orchards as well. It was also known for its swamps and unsettling soil, but it had huge cotton fields.

We'd pack ourselves into Daddy's car. He was a Ford man. During that time and for years to come, he drove a Ford. Mama and Daddy and one of us kids sat up front. The rest of us were in the back seat. Mama packed food and clothes for our two-day trip. We had baloney and crackers, kool-aide, and water. Mama had fried chicken and "light bread" for dinner. (Light bread was another name for Wonder Bread.)

"Make sure you all share that baloney back there. We got enough crackers for everyone, so stop all that bickering back there. You hear me? Odell's gonna stop in a few minutes so you can get out and use the bathroom. We're almost there, so settle down."

After a short distance, Daddy would pull over on the side of the highway and we kids got out and used the bathroom alongside the road. I squatted and peed. The boys went off and peed in the bushes.

Dos Palos is located in Merced County in northern California. We'd drive for hours in the dark and arrive just before daybreak to get our cotton sacks and get assigned to a row.

If you knew what you were doing, you'd get two sacks and pick cotton from both sides of the row. Some of the veteran cotton pickers could do that. We were not that skilled.

On those occasions when Mama's mother, Lila, met us at

the cotton field, she always got two sacks. That woman could pick from both sides of the row with no problem. She was good, really good.

Mama and Daddy were fairly good cotton pickers. My older brothers, Alfred, Odell, and Donell were average pickers. Me and my younger brother, Glenn, were not so good. In fact, we were bad. I tried to do my best, but at age seven or eight, I was just not equipped to do the work.

At the end of the day when I took my cotton sack to the truck to be weighed, I knew the scale needle would not move that much. I usually made just enough money to buy myself a soda and a candy bar.

We'd work all day Saturday, and sleep in the car that night. We'd get up early Sunday morning and work all day until evening. We'd pack ourselves into Daddy's Ford and return home late Sunday night. We were tired, dirty, and exhausted after two days in the cotton patch. But it was during those weekends that we kids felt like a family, because Daddy was spending time with us.

OAKLAND, CALIFORNIA

Our family moved to Oakland in the mid-50s. I must have been eight or nine years old. Daddy's job transferred him to a Naval division in Martinez. Martinez is a city in the San Francisco Bay Area. It's about seventeen miles from Oakland.

We started a new chapter in our lives. Gone were the days of living in a small town. No more could a neighbor say, "Run to the store, baby, and get me some cigarettes and a can of beer. Take this note with you." No

My brothers Donell, Glenn, and Odell

more running barefoot into the night and playing until we were exhausted. Now, we were in the big city. We had to be home when the streetlights came on.

Mama found work as a domestic. She cleaned houses for rich, white folks. She would talk to us about her employers. She said some were petty and stingy. But some of the women treated Mama with respect; they gave her lovely, expensive clothes they no longer wore. They even sat and discussed politics and current events with her at lunch. One employer even wanted her opinion on some opera she was going to attend. They realized Mama was poor, but she was also intelligent.

Mama talked to us kids about her mean employers. "They won't allow me to even open the refrigerator to get water. Most families allow me to make my lunch with whatever is on hand. In some homes, I'm not allowed to touch any of their food. I must bring my own lunch." I can only imagine the indignities Mama endured and didn't tell us.

Mama worked in various homes in Lafayette, Piedmont, Walnut Creek, and Orinda. She took at least 2 to 3 buses to get to her jobs. After working 8-9 hours, she boarded 2 to 3 buses to head home. But before coming home, many a day, Mama had to stop and get groceries.

Daddy continued to stay gone all weekend. He continued to be reckless with his money. He continued to abuse Mama when the guilt was too much for him.

Oakland opened up new worlds for the Berry family. My brother, Alfred, became obsessed with the tenor saxophone; that was his first love. He studied music and eventually joined a rock 'n roll band called *Johnny Hartsman and the Rhythm Rockers*. He even toured the United States with that group. Alfred introduced the family to music. We began listening to the sounds of John Coltrane, Dexter Gordon, Cannonball Adderley, Miles Davis, Nina Simone, Thelonious Monk, and so many more. Our apartment was filled with sounds I'd never heard before.

Alfred even began "processing" his hair for "show business." He was introduced to this chemical process whereby his naturally kinky hair would miraculously become relaxed, or as we called it — straight. The twins, always the adventurous ones, thought they would try this new style and straighten their hair at home with lye.

They proudly wore a "conk." A few times, one of the twins left the lye in their hair too long and you could hear screaming all over the neighborhood as they tried to shampoo each other's burning scalps.

Mama introduced me to Royal Crown Hairdressing and the hot comb. Many a Saturday morning, Mama held me captive, pressing my hair with the hot comb. As she blew on my neck, she'd say, "Hold your ear, baby, while I get a little closer." I must say, I did look a lot different wearing my hair pressed. I no longer wore my natural hair in braids. Oh, no. I was sportin' a ponytail now.

Lack of supervision introduced me to liquor. Alfred and his fellow musicians practiced at our house often. We had an old piano in the front room and Alfred, General, Cotton, and Fred practiced long and hard on Saturdays. When they were spent, they'd leave the house with only their instruments. They left behind a treasure of half- empty malt liquor cans and ashtrays full of half-smoked cigarettes. I didn't smoke, but I enjoyed the malt liquor. My brother, Glenn, and I always volunteered to clean up after they left. Mama was busy cooking and washing on the weekends. Daddy, of course, was gone.

The twins began having problems with the law. They eventually went to juvenile hall for long periods. My mother would visit them by bus on the weekends. I loved school, so that kept me busy. My younger brother, Glenn, was finding his way in life. He was always well-liked. He and his friends stayed just shy of breaking any laws.

Then one night our lives changed. Once again, Mama and Daddy had started arguing over the lack of money coming in. Daddy got angry and, eventually, started punching Mama. Bruised and battered, she left for her own safety. She found shelter at a friend's house. She left so quickly, we didn't go with her.

The next day, Daddy found out where she was staying and went to her, trying to sweet-talk her into returning. Mama had left for the umpteenth time, but this time she was determined to change her life. I was told she took off one shoe — a shoe with a big, thick heel and she began beating Daddy in the head with all her might. She beat Daddy until he stumbled to the ground. She beat him for all the black eyes he had given her, for all the bruises he had put on her body, for all the indignities she had suffered. Daddy was stunned, shocked, and had to be taken to the hospital for medical treatment.

After years of physical and emotional abuse, Mama finally decided to leave my father. She got the nerve to get a divorce. We kids were ecstatic. I was around thirteen at the time.

She held her head high as a single mother raising five kids on her own. After the divorce, Daddy married three more times. Time eventually matured him. He came to Mama one day and apologized. He realized he had done wrong. The times were against him. He later became a highly respected man in his community of Pittsburgh where he was an elder at a local church. As an adult, when I visited him, people (white and Black) would tell me how honorable he was and how well he treated people.

My brother, Bo, went on to become an interstate trucker, with a wife, a beautiful home in Texas, and the owner of some income property. Alfred went on to become an engineer for the postal service. He and his wife purchased a lovely home in the Oakland hills. My brother, Odell, became a regional manager in northern California with the Employment Development Department. My brother, Donell, became a manager at a cable company in northern California. I went on to become a Social Worker, and later, a Parole Agent. I developed a passion for acting and writing and now I'm headed down those trails. My younger brother, Glenn, went on to become a Captain at the Oakland Fire Department.

I don't believe witnessing domestic violence left any visible scars. My brothers and I have settled down and lead relatively normal lives. We remain close to this day. Our bond is strong. Our mother set a good example for us on how to conduct ourselves. We experienced pain, but we are resilient.

Mama and Daddy are no longer on this plane. They have joined our ancestors. These two people lived their lives the best they could in the era they were born into. They were both broken by the times in which they lived. Daddy was looking for respect and his manhood. Mama was looking for a better world in which to raise her children. I'm guessing she was also looking for love and affection. I believe we all were looking for a better day.

LOOKING BACK...

I now understand some of the pitfalls of being Black in America. Being held down in America's racial caste system was a way of life for us. I guess we were all waiting for that day when things would be better. We were all waiting for that *"someday"*. But "someday" is not on the calendar.

My parents had hopes and dreams. But what happens to dreams deferred? Langston Hughes explained it. They fester and eventually explode. For many of us, our dreams are festering.

My parents wanted a better life. Like so many, they struggled to survive in a place and time that could not – would not — allow them to have the "American dream." They struggled while waiting and searching for a better way, a better day. They may have taken some wrong turns, but haven't we all?

My father, Odell Berry, and me

About the Author: Patricia Forté
Teacher / Actress / Author

Patricia has been a member of the Screen Actors Guild (SAG) and the American Federation of Television and Radio Artists (AFTRA) for over twenty years. She has appeared on stage, screen, and television. She has worked as a voice over artist on radio with First Lady Barbara Bush and actor/director/playwright Ted Lange.

Patricia has taught creative writing and drama at various middle schools in Los Angeles and the San Fernando Valley. She taught drama for ten years at the K-C Theatre Arts School in Hollywood. She went on to teach creative writing to at-risk youth at Kittsville Youth Foundation. This program was founded by the legendary actress/social activist, Eartha Kitt.

Ms. Forté is the author of *The Cambridge Way*, a book chronicling Black theatre from the Harlem Renaissance to the year 2000. She is also the author of *All Aboard* (currently being edited). This book takes a candid look at an enslaved group of women who, against the odds, help others escape the horrors of slavery.

THREE

MY SAVIOR, DR. MARGARET G. BURROUGHS

Odie Hawkins

1948

Chicago has four distinctive sides: the Northside, the Southside, the Westside, and Lake Michigan, east. Each section has a slumghetto. Way back in 1937, I was born in the Westside slumghetto, "Jewtown" (so named by the Jewish merchants who did their "bidness" there), and I lived, survived, at one point or another, in the other slumghettos. We moved a lot.

'Round about the time, I was six or seven, it seemed that something woke up in me that alerted me to the fact that life was not sweet and juicy. Instead, it was mostly the opposite.

I will never be able to identify what it was that stirred this feeling around in me. Maybe it was when I first realized that I didn't own a coat that really kept me warm in the winter. And, as everybody knows, it can get very cold in Chicago.

I was eight when my Daddy was sentenced to three to five in Statesville Penitentiary, Joliet, Illinois. I wouldn't see him unbarred again 'til I was thirteen.

My Daddy ("Father makes you do; Daddy lets you do. I'm yo' Daddy."), a proud Black petty criminal, had turned down the "opportunity" to be freed after serving three years and put on parole for another two years.

"I don't want to be reportin' to some White man every week for two years."

So, The System accommodated him by retaining him for two more years and a bonus eight months. Five years and eight months for a ten dollar ($10.00) stick-up. It was unfair, but I didn't recognize "unfair" at the time; it was just what it was.

Yeah, I was about eight when life seemed to become really real for me. My Momma was "out in the streets" while Daddy was doing his time. I don't think it would've mattered much if he had been out of the slams and she hadn't been "out in the streets," because they weren't really together when they were together. Later, after I had studied their stuff closely, I came to the conclusion that they had always had a feral relationship.

She was sixteen and he was eighteen when they got married. I copied the City Hall contract. She was one of the displaced persons who had been terrorized out of Helena, Arkansas, by the local racists. Ditto for Daddy's family out of Yazoo City, Mississippi.

They had me out of sexual passion (and my sister, too) and didn't want to be married. Ray Charles and Stevie Wonder could've seen that. Who wants to have their street time cut off by midnight feedings?

For years after Daddy served his time, I could count on seeing him whenever he felt like seeing my Momma. Yeah, it was feral. Whenever they got together, they were always physically fighting or doin' this nude wrestlin' thing that I witnessed as often as I saw him.

And then he'd be off again. And we would be left in some dark, dank hole in the wall, waiting for Momma to come back with something to eat. Or, we would be stashed with a relative somewhere. Through all of it, from kindergarten onward, I was sent to school—*childcare* for the needy.

I actually went to 17 grammar schools. I used to be able to remember their names in chronological order, but I'm jumping a bit ahead of myself. From one slumghetto to another slumghetto. That was the pattern. We never questioned why this was happening, we just went along with the program. One of the most vivid memories

I have of the places we survived in and out of, was our three- to-four years' stay in Aint Mary's basement: 1150 W. Washburne, right on the fringe of "Jewtown," Maxwell and Halstead Streets.

I still have no idea why we wound up living in this spot for so long. Maybe it had something to do with Aint Mary being my Daddy's oldest sister. Children didn't question adults about anything back then. Aint Mary's basement was warm (*there was a potbellied coal stove in the all-purpose/ kitchen area, which was converted to a gambling casino/craps on Friday and Saturday—and, until Aint Mary went to the Rev. A.T. Tilley's Sunrise Baptist Church, the doors east of us, on Sunday morning*) and full of rats.

The rats outnumbered us by the thousands. In the winter, seeking mammal warmth, they surreptitiously snuggled up between our inner thighs. You could tell where they had spent some time under the cover from looking at the rat tracks and small, black, shit pellets they had left behind.

The summers were even worse. Maybe they had a birth surge or something in the Spring, but, by the time the humid Chicago summers settled in on us, the rats were prowling the alleys in packs, herds. I actually hated to go to bed, because these watermelon rind-fed, bar-b-que bone-fattened rodents became so ebullient, so effervescently active; they would run across my body in the middle of the night, playing tag or whatever.

One of my most realistic nightmares was a large grey rat pausing on my chest, resting himself from his strenuous play on my cot, his beady eyes challenging me to question his right to be resting on my chest. I don't know how long he stayed there, but I've felt the weight of his body on my chest ever since then.

We were jammed together on Washbourne Avenue, like rats in a cage, which often gave birth to outrageous behavior. Husbands beat their wives. Wives razored their abusive spouse's throats in their sleep. Boys and girls were whipped with razor straps for childish behavior. Feuds between family clans ebbed and flowed. Only the fittest could survive.

The men who came down into Aint Mary's gambling house (Friday to Sunday mornings, when she took time to garb herself in her Rev. A.T. Tilley's Sunrise Baptist Church Usherette/Deaconess uniform), hoping to "break the bank," were also guilty of as much negative behavior as they could get away with on her turf.

"Awright, Mule Poppa, I done tol' you 'n Frenchy to stop usin' all that bad language up in heah. We got cherren sleepin' in the front room."

The whole scene was semi-bipolar. Below the negativity, there were feelings so deep and loving, so warm and sympathetic, it seemed that I was being bathed in a kind of love that no one else in America could ever experience. Or imagine.

"Son, you wont a piece of this sweet patater pie I just made?"

"Yes Ma'am, Miss Rabbit, I sure do. And thank you, Ma'am."

Thousands of moments like that counterattacked the other stuff.

"Awright lil' nigga! Gimme yo' money or your life!" Going to jail, to the Big House, to the Joint, to the Slams was considered an element of our rite of passage. I can remember dudes calling across our crowded streets to each other ...

"Hey nigga! Is you done did yo' time yet?"

My Daddy, recently released, tried to prep me for a brighter future ...

"Go 'head on, do what you gon' do, but don't get caught; the penitentiary is hard on a motherfucker's soul." Awright, that's enough of that. I've edited myself around huge mounds of blood, sweat, tears, emotional scenes so deep that it might even cause unfeeling White folks to understand what I've written, what we feel.

$$\bigstar \bigstar \bigstar \bigstar \bigstar$$

I don't know why (lots of "I don't know whys" up in here) we wound up living in the Almo Hotel for four consecutive years. It was sort of a strange record. After years of being shuttled from Ain't Mary's basement to Uncle Eddie's basement (on the Northside, where I ran out in the street between two parked cars, smack dab into the passenger side of a chauffeur-driven limo. I lived, the car was badly dented) back to Ain't Mary's basement for a few months. And then onward to Ain't Mamie's basement. Basements were cheaper. To somewhere else. We (Momma and sister) moved from place to place so fast it seems like a blurred memory.

"Y'all don't live in this room no mo'. Yo' momma tol' me to give you this. This is yall's new address."

The Almo Hotel. I was fifteen. I had graduated from Forestville Grammar School, attending on a fake address. And now, incredibly, I was going to go on to high school. "You may have to walk to school if you want to go."

I started paying closer attention to my nomadic life. I would definitely have to have a permanent address to go to high school, the rules determined that. I don't know how she did it, but come school time, I was a registered freshie at Du Sable High School, with 3800 S. Lake Park Avenue as my address.

We were still moving from place to place in all of the slumghettos in the city, but the Almo Hotel (It wasn't really a hotel anymore. A semi-brothel would be a more honest description.) became our "home." The Almo Hotel had once been a fashionable four-story building. It was something else when we occupied our two rooms on the third floor, with two windows facing a big vacant lot.

The first floor was strictly for the hoe-soldiers who marched in and out 24/7 with their tricks. Ditto for the second floor. The action was bombastic on the weekends.

The third floor was half "Army" and half "Civilian".

The fourth floor was reserved for off-duty hoe-soldiers and reclining pimp officers. Heroin was the drug of choice for the dope fiends who roamed the dark carpeted passageways, noddin' off in the toilets. "Everything was everything", to quote the late, great, Donny Hathaway. I ran errands for the "soldiers" on the fourth floor and, during the course of my time around them, learned many of their sexual tricks.

"They be thinkin' they got it in, but they ain't got nothin' in nowhere. They just be pumpin' jissum between my thighs…"

Big Al, the pimp with the suits that shined in the night, took me under his wing for a few months. He ran his "Game" down to me.

"You got a whole bunch of games to run on a potential candidate for your stable: You got some emotionally dehydrated women out there, who just searching for a drink. You become her drink, dig what I'm sayin'? You got some women who are searching for their Daddies. You become their Daddy, and you charge them for your time. You got weak sisters who can't refuse your demands. You got, you got, you got an endless supply of hoe-soldiers (see the real meaning of "Hoe"?) out there who are just dyin' to go to the battlefield for you. All you have to learn how to do is motivate them."

I flunked pimpin' 101 because I could not force myself to ask some female to go sell her body for me. Big Al always looked at me in a snarky way after he discovered my "weakness," but he never righteously condemned me. All he said in passing, at one point, was: "Any woman can be a hoe, but it takes a special kind of man to be a pimp."

✳ ✳ ✳ ✳ ✳

Momma was right. I did have to walk to Du Sable a lot.

If I had a few coins, I had to make a decision.

Should I spend the money on bus fare or save it for a bag of potato chips and a Coca-Cola lunch? I always chose to walk because I knew I would be able to steal something to eat enroute to school. Or, I could steal something at school. I was stealing quite a bit right in thru here.

I practically ravaged the purses and pocketbooks of the luscious young ladies of Du Sable. I hope there is a statute of limitations. If they laid it down anywhere near me, I had it.

If they left their lockers open and turned their backs, I was in it. Couple this with the pilfered pork chops and 'loney meat that I was slipping into my pants from the markets I visited on a rotational basis. I could say that I was feeding my family pretty well.

We became almost affluent when I created the "love letter writing bidness." Here is exactly what happened. I'm strolling thru the upper level of the school with a buddy, looking for something to rip off. My buddy has other ideas. "I sho' would like some of them panties."

"Huh?" His other thoughts and ideas jarred me from my larcenous reveries.

He nodded with his chin at this gorgeous creature swaying past us on the other side of the hallway. Truth be told, they had some of the most gorgeous girl-women at Du Sable than any other school in the city. They were gorgeous, sexy, and approachable. It was a great plus to know how to write a "Love Note."

I don't really know how that came about. I think it may have had something to do with the times, the era. Nat "King" Cole was romancing our minds with "Mona Lisa".

Sarah Vaughn was embracing us with lyricism. Billie, Bird, Pres, Miles, Diz, Do Wop, and Be-Bop ran parallel races. I actually went to parties where people were reading Gwendolyn Brooks, Langston Hughes, and Do Bop She Bam.

In any case, like I said, it was a plus to know how to write a "Love Note". Girls at Du Sable expected to be hit on by notes. That was the way it was.

"Why don't you write 'Miss Gorgeous' a note?" I asked my buddy.

"I don't know how to write none of that stuff."

I looked at him. He was serious. Willie could've been the first Lou Rawls, but he could barely spell his own name. Maybe he was dyslectic or something. I butted in.

"I'll write the note for you…." "You will?!"

"What did I just say?" "When?" "Tomorrow."

There, I had cornered myself, nothing to do but go to work. I started putting some sort of outline together as I jog-walked back to the Almo that evening. I knew "Miss Gorgeous" as a familiar stranger. Everybody knew everybody, one way or another, at Du

Sable. How many were we? Two-thousand odd? A small village. We knew most of the people in our class sets. I was entering my sophomore year when my Love Letter writing really took off. The letter that I wrote for Willie got him an audition that he flunked.

"Look, I got to give it to you, man, that note you wrote for me really impressed her, but I didn't. I mean, she wanted to go to the Peps to see the latest movies 'n' shit like that. And I had to tell her that I couldn't handle that kind of program. So, that's where we left it."

That was it for him, but the beginning for me. I made a path to the boutique "Love Letter Writing bidness." It went like this: I charged a dollar for an ordinary. Two dollars for a "special". Three dollars for an "exotic". And, four dollars for an "outrageous". They had to re-write what I wrote in their own handwriting and let me see it before they passed it to her.

I glared around for competitors. I didn't have any. I had a clear field 'til I was in my third year – my junior year – when an unexpected emotional earthquake messed me up. I'll get to that. Now, here are examples of the four "genres" I wrote in when my Love Letter ballpoint was hot—and only for carefully-screened clients.

#1 The Ordinary – $1.00

My name is Jason Smack,

I'm the guy sitting two desks behind you in English 201, Mrs. Pace's class. I can't begin to tell you how much time I spend thinking of how wonderful it would be to have a desk that faced you every day. This note does not come out of the blue, off the top of my head. I've thought about a half-dozen ways I wanted to approach you, to ask you if you would like to go to the lunchroom with me, or spend a few minutes just walking around the school, just talking. To be honest, what all of this comes down to is that I would like to get to know you, to know something about your hopes, your dreams your future. I hope you don't think that I'm being too brash, too full of myself to even think that someone as wonderful as you would give me a play. But, as my mother is always saying, "Nothing beats a failure but a try." I'm

trying...Please feel free to let me know what you think of this note when I see you after class tomorrow.
   Your friendly admirer,
   Jason Smack

My literary ego was jacked sky high when I saw my boy J. and Miss Cutie Pie –whatshername–moon strolling down the hall two days later. My mojo was working.

#2 The Special – $2.00

Dear Shirlene Adams,
This has gone far enough, me trying to hold my feelings about you in check. As you know, there comes a time in every man's life when he has to push the macho mask off to one side and let his feelings show, to be for real. Can you dig where I'm coming from? I know you are a popular young lady 'cause I see all the attention people (especially the males) be giving you. But I notice that you don't seem to have a big head, you remain your calm, beautiful self. I like that, I like that very much. I've spent a few days trying to figure out the best way I could bring myself into your inner circle, to have you understand that I see you as a special girl. So, you see, there it is. I'm revealing my feelings for you. You may reject my attention, but I hope you won't. I hope that you will be available to go to ShakeBaby's birthday party. This coming Saturday, "ShakeBaby" made it a point to tell all of us who had a special invitation to bring our "Special Ladies". I'm asking you to go to "ShakeBaby's" with me as my "Special Lady." I would also like to say, "ShakeBaby" or no "ShakeBaby", that I always think of you as a "Special Lady."
   Very Affectionately yours,
   Garry S. Scott

More egoistic ratings. Hey, I was doin' this! It got to the point where I was willing to guarantee "success" or refund the fee paid.

#3 The Exotic coming right up – $3.00

My Darling Mamie,
When I say your name out loud it makes me think of balmy tropical

breezes, gently waving palm trees, body warm ocean waves. When I see you sway thru the hallway, on your way to your locker, or wherever, I take lascivious notice of the rhythmic motions of your hips, the proud way you hold your head as you glance at the people all around you. I've often heard people talk about what it felt like to be hypnotized, fascinated by forces beyond their control. I feel that way about you. I know we've only had three or four conversations standing beside our lockers, but each time we've talked made me feel a deeper fascination. It's as though I wanted to kiss your lips as each word escaped your mouth. I cannot remember what we talked about, but I do recall the shape your beautiful lips made as the words came out. Please don't think that it's only your lips that I'm interested in. I'm interested in all of you. And I want you to consider my offer to become interested in me also.

Let's talk about it very soon,
Affectionately, forever,
Le Roi Wilson"

#4 The Outrageous – $4.00

"Look, baby, I have to get up between them sweet honeypot thighs. That's what my passion streak whispers into my brain every time I see you. You didn't have no panties on yesterday. You know how I could tell? Well, I'm not going to tell you, I'll have to show you. It's really a sin 'n' a shame that I have to put my desire for you into writing. I know every time you look into my eyes, you know my freak is on for you. Why don't you just be honest and admit that you want the same thing I want, that orgasmic thrill that's going to blow both of our minds? What I want you to do, when you get through reading this, is come up to me, no matter where I am, no matter what I'm doing, and whisper in my left ear. My left ear – "Bobby, I wanna give you some this evening." That's all you got to say. I'll take care of the place and the time.

Love and mo' love,
Bobby Franklin"

No bullshit. I was workin' it until that unexpected emotional earthquake messed me all up, that I spoke of earlier. There I was, strolling thru the first-floor hallway, minding my own bidness, "Contracts" to do – three "Outrageouses" in my notebook.

I looked into these pop-bottle bottomed eyeglasses, mounted on this beautiful sculptured broad nose. A Black girl. I mean, a real Black girl, not one of those February month-Negro History month-Black girls. She was small, couldn't've been taller than five feet, and was perfectly proportioned. No big ol' boody and big ol' titties, or nothing like. Everything was exactly the size and shape it was supposed to be. I stopped and stared at her. She rewarded me with a quick, friendly smile. That was it.

Secretly, to tell the honest to God truth, I think I had a lot of internal smirking goin' on about these brothers who were buying "Love Letters" from me. I thought it was kind of funny, 'til I saw Sola strolling thru the hall. Who was she? Where did she come from? I felt I had to get to know her. I felt like I wanted her.

This was a totally new feeling for me. I spent the whole day in a sort of daze, trying to figure out how to get to her. It only took one visit to the office to learn that this stopper was named Sola Gray and she was from someplace called Hackensack, New Jersey. Just transferred in.

My days after that became a kind of Sola blur. I would spot her in an A.K.A. formation and then she would be gone, off to math or gym or wherever. She was elusive. I would position myself in one place and she would disappear from another place. I was still doing letters for my "clients," but I was definitely thinking of a "Master Letter" that I wanted to write.

I didn't know what it was that drew me to her. Well, let me qualify that. I definitely wanted to get in them panties. That was the teenager in me. But then, there were other thoughts brewing. I could see her as my wife, the mother of our two children, Taiwo and Kehinde. I had read enough stuff about African names to know that we would probably have twins that we would call "Taiwo" and "Kehinde".

Meanwhile, with all of this drippin' drama blundering through my skull, I was still doing bidness.

"Awright, Eddie, who do you want to address this to?" "Let's call her... 'Lady Mysterious'.

"Lady Mysterious, huh? That sounds pretty mysterious to me – Outrageous?"

"Naww, this is 'Exotic'. Let's make it 'Exotic'."

"Exotic? That sounds just right for a 'Lady Mysterious' – three dollars please."

Awright, the brother wanted his 'Exotic' addressed to "Lady Mysterious". So be it. I didn't give a shit, I was focused on my agenda with Sola. No doubt in my mind that she would have to dig me. I didn't have any outsized markers (I wasn't tall, dark, and handsome), but I had been nurtured in the pimp tradition of – "Yo' pussy cain't be good less my dick says it is...."

I was anxious to put some avant-garde concepts to work. Meanwhile...

I'm in Teacher Burroughs's art class. It's supposed to be one of the classes you needed on your card to graduate, so I was in Teacher Burroughs's art class. Let me chop this off right here to say something about Teacher Burroughs, later to be known as Dr. Margaret G. Burroughs.

<u>An Aside</u>: Teacher Burroughs, later to be known as Dr. Margaret G. Burroughs, was one of the most Afrocentric art educators in the Chicago Public School system. No doubt in my mind that some racist White bureaucrat made a major league mistake when he allowed her to teach at Du Sable.

Du Sable, a high school in ghettoslum bound Chicago, a place that was supposed to be doomed by its name alone – "Du Sable!" "A high school named after a Negro?! What kind of nonsense is this?!"

My guess is that they located their mistake too late. I won't even try to identify all of the Afrocentrists who plunged into the Du Sable ocean. They came to us loaded with Langston Hughes shells, Zora Neale Hurston guns, different ways of looking at ourselves.

They've put the "Renaissance Series", or whatever the latest TV series wants to call Anglo America's attempt to co-opt African-American 'Ourstory.' No good, White folks. You got to start at Dr. Margaret G. Burroughs. Dr. B. established the first Museum of

African American History in the U.S. Why is that a problem for people to see/hear/ understand?

Well, one of the reasons why is that she was such a Bitch. She bitched Left, Center, and Right. And eventually got what she most bitched for – the Du Sable Museum of African-American History. Her bitching was so powerful that we don't even have a PBS Series or any other shout- out for identification of what she did. Now, that's what I call a real bitchin! – End of Aside,

Teacher Burroughs, a seasoned collector of illicit student papers, leaned over behind my furiously scribbling ballpoint, to gently pluck a half-written "Exotic" off of my desk. Damn! A hip lady, she knew how to get beyond a would-be cheater and corner him at the pass.

That's what she did to me. The bell rang, signaling a class change.

"Don't go, I want to talk with you." That's what she said, as my classmates filed out, throwing darts at my predicament. Damn!

"Gotcha ass, huh?"

She didn't waste a minute. She sat at her desk and gestured for me to sit at the desk in front of her. She sat there, looking dead into my face for a long minute before she leaned over and started writing. She spoke to me after she finished writing.

"I've written a note to my friend Margaret Petersen, who has a creative writing class on Friday, at 6 p.m., at the Baptist Institute. You know where that is?"

"Uhhh, yes Ma'am. 51st and South Parkway, right across from the park."

"Good. Go there, with this note on Friday at 6. If you don't attend the class, I will fail you. And you will have to make up Art 101 to graduate."

There it was, threat and blackmail all rolled into one. Sister could be cold, cold, cold. She handed me the pages (Remember? Three pages for the "Exotic". Three dollars.), and her comment.

"I teach our Black people to appreciate our unique place in this society. I'm not a writing instructor, but I do read a lot, and I think that what you've written here is very fine, excellent."

I stood there in front of her desk, on the verge of crying. Teacher Burroughs had certified my stuff. My first thought was – I got to jack up my prices.

✳ ✳ ✳ ✳ ✳

I have to admit that I was shocked, really shocked to find that Mrs. Petersen, Teacher Burroughs' friend, was a White woman. An ugly White woman with mousy blonde hair, Bunny Rabbit upper fronts, Gypsy clothes on her back, and just like Teacher Burroughs, a cold, cold, cold sister.

"Let's understand something clearly. You're in this class because Margaret has asked me to admit you. I'm not after quantity, I insist on quality. And that's that."

Imagine a buck-toothed White woman saying something like that at the Baptist Institute, on 51st and South Parkway, a 6 p.m. on Friday, in 1953? Sister was bold, bold, bold. There were twenty people in the class when I was admitted, five of us, and fifteen of them. Six weeks later, there were ten of them and two of us. I felt compelled to explain why I had dropped out to Teacher Burroughs.

"I just can't keep up." It was wintertime.

"Boy! Why didn't you tell me that you were walking from 38th and Lake Park to get to school?"

I didn't know what to say. I had been walking/jogging for almost three years. So, what's the Big Deal? Now, I discovered the warm, warm, warm side of Teacher Burroughs.

"Well, because of extenuating circumstances, I'm not going to fail you. But, when we break for the summer so-called vacation, I'm going to give you a ream of paper and I want you to come back here in September with a novel. Or else I'm going to have to fail you. Are we clear on this?" "Yes, Ma'am." I never knew what to say to Teacher Burroughs, other than "Yes, Ma'am". Meanwhile, I had a hot hand going with my love letter bidness. Like I said, following Teacher Burroughs' endorsement (news traveled fast), I had upped each of my categories by a buck. I didn't think a whole lot about this brother, who requested an "Exotique-Exotique", without any "nastiness" in it.

"What do you call 'Nasty', my brother?" "You know, all that stuff referring to sex." "So, what's wrong with that?"

"Well, this is goin' to a Christian girl. I'm a Christian boy." Fuck it. I didn't have any qualms about writing a straight- up – I want you, baby – Christian appeal for the brother. Meanwhile, I'm still semi-stalking Sola Gray.

"Who you want to address this *none 'nasty'* letter to, my brother?" I reached the point of being sarcastic toward all levels of Black-niss.

"I want it addressed to Christian Lady."

No problem, "Christian Lady", here we come. No pun intended.

I did the "Christian Lady" letter as efficiently as I had ever done any other "Love Letter". The difference, I think, is that my brief attendance in Margaret "Buck teeth" Petersen's class had taught me the reasons for an emphasis on character profiles, motivation, clear definitions, and a certain sense of style. Style, an almost undefinable way of writing about things in a certain way. Try to imagine Doris Day trying to sing any song that Billie Holiday, Sarah Vaughn, Carmen McCrea, Ella, Nina, Bessie, 'Retha, Mahalia, Ochun, or whoever comes out of that Gospel tradition.

Please remember, the stuff I'm stuffin' you with happened sixty-some years ago, back in ancient times.

(Recall that the "Love Letters" the Undergroundmaster wrote for his "Clients" were copied, per his demand, in the "Client's" own handwriting. This created some interesting problems years later when some of the recipients of those "Love Letters" outed the whole scene. "Do you really think that I thought Melvin wrote that letter to me? Back then, my husband couldn't even spell half the words in that letter.")

I stopped writing the "Love Letters" when one of the "Letters" backfired on me. This was the "Exotic" that Teacher Burroughs caught, being directed at "Lady Mysterious". The letter was going from my friend Eddie to Sola Gray. I didn't know that then. I didn't really connect things 'til I saw Eddie "moon walkin'" thru the first-floor hallway with my heart stroke-to-be, this wonderful creature that I wanted in my life so desperately.

I damned near fainted when I saw them together. I had hooked Eddie up with my Love. And it was obvious from the way they were looking at each other, that a fire had been lit. I didn't cry, truth be told. Well, I didn't cry right then, but I did cry. I went into a wounded shell. I had to turn down requests for my work.

"Exotic, where you at, brother?" I tried to write a few letters, but I just couldn't put my heart into the effort. My heart was broken.

I stayed in a depressed state for a long time (about two months – a lifetime for a fifteen-sixteen-year-old). I just couldn't see my way out of the blues 'til I decided to unburden myself to Teacher Burroughs. She was unusually sympathetic. She even offered me a way to deal with my heartbreak.

"The summer break is two weeks away. I'm going to give you a ream of paper. I want you to write about what it feels like to have your heart broken. Let me see what you've written when we come back in September."

"Yes, Ma'am."

I think her advice (and all that paper) was a release agent for me. Please remember, this happened sixty-some years ago, back in ancient times. A number of things started changing my head as I started writing that summer. Number one, I stopped stealing (so much) after I had a whole week of nightmares featuring me and two buffed-up convicts in a small cell with a jar of Vaseline.

Come September, I presented Teacher Burroughs with a hand-scribbled manuscript: my first novel, the story of a young man's heartbreak. Since that time, I've written a number of other novels, none of them about heartbreak. If I had written more novels about heartbreak since that time, I would have a whole library shelf filled with self- indulgence and morbid thoughts. That ain't what's happenin'.

LOOKING BACK...

...over these influential years, I appreciate those experiences which caused me to be the Odie Hawkins of today. In closing the generation gap, I echo the words of Dr. Dre (hip hop icon) when I say, "You just have to find that thing that's special about you that distinguishes you from all others, and through true talent, hard work, and passion, anything can happen."

About the Author: Odie Hawkins
Author / Certified Tai Chi Instructor

Odie Hawkins was encouraged by Alex Haley in the 1980's when he told Norman Lear, "I think Odie Hawkins is a very talented writer, a brilliant storyteller. He deserves a wider audience." Odie Hawkins, working with Alex Haley, wrote the teleplay for "Old Sister". S. Pearl Sharp as Saundra Sharp, wrote the story. "Old Sister" aired on CBS in the *Palmerstown* television drama series. Norman Lear and Alex Haley, based the series on their own childhoods. (imdb.com/title/ tt0668946/). Invigorated by Dr. Margaret Burroughs, Budd Schulberg, Louise Meriwether, John W. Bloch, Al Jenner, Robert Lewin, Harlan Ellison and Professor Justin Gifford, Odie Hawkins continues to write. We hear his love for stories in his radio plays (archive.org/details/ OTRR_Sears_Radio_Theater_Singles).

We acknowledge his diverse experiences in documentaries – "Iceberg Slim: Portrait of a Pimp" (Director Jorge Hinojosa) and "Burn Motherf*cker Burn" (by Sacha Jenkins). Facebook and YouTube provide more insight on this talented author, musician, and actor.

Odie Hawkins has been given the title, "The Underground Master", by a loyal constituency who have followed his career through his thirty-two novels, short story collections, essays, television scripts, radio and film scripts. He takes pride in being the originator of the Pan- African Occult genre, as exemplified by

"The Snake, 20/ 20", "Shackles Across Time" and "The Snake Doctor".

He was one of the original members of the famed Watts Writers Workshop, established by Budd Schulberg, in the wake of the Watts Rebellion, 1965; and the Open Door Program, created by the Writers Guild of America, West, Inc. Louise Meriwether, John W. Bloch, Al Jenner, Robert Lewin, Harlan Ellison and Budd Schulberg, instructors. *"Ghetto Sketches"*, his first published novel, was on the required reading list – May 2010 – Professor Justin Gifford; University of Nevada, Reno, Department of English. Mr. Hawkins has also recently published books of Socio- Science fiction: *"Lady Bliss"* (with co-author Ralph Vernon), and *"Mr. Bonobo Bliss aka Bo"*.

Mr. Odie Hawkins' current projects are: "A Story Teller's Tale", an update on "The Chicago Sista" and political satire.

odiehawkins.com
linkedin.com/in/ odie-hawkins-044633a/
facebook.com/odie.hawkins

FOUR

IMPRINTING MY SOUL

Zola Salena-Hawkins

1950

A loud creaking sound — sounds as the door is flung open. Yes, I recall that is the first loud noise I ever heard. I was standing in my crib, after throwing out the empty milk can. It was a brown and orange can — maybe a Hire's root beer can with a nipple on it. "Mama White" (my maternal grandmother) had creatively fashioned a makeshift bottle with this can and a rubber nipple because I had successfully broken all the glass bottles. When the bottle was empty, I would simply throw it as far as my little arms could throw.

I was standing there wondering where are my people? You know, those folks that I saw on a daily basis. There were my biological parents, Frank Victor Johnson, Jr. aka "Father," and Helen Jewel aka "Mother Dear" that I had known since birth.

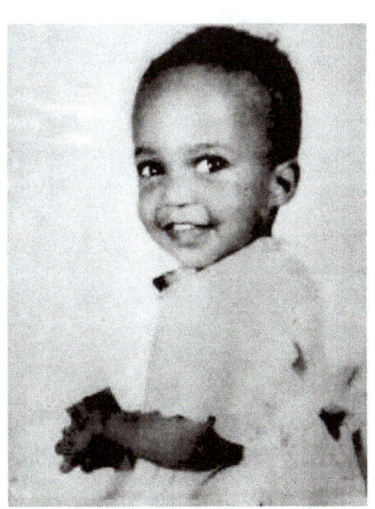

Zola, about 2 years old

Because my father was rarely at home and my mother was away attending nursing school at Fairleigh Dickinson University in the nearby town of Teaneck, New Jersey, I learned early to refer to my maternal grandparents — Rev. John Westly White as "Daddy" and Salena-Philpot White as "Mama". (Please note, in my twenties, I learned that my cousins called them "Daddy White" and "Mama White").

We all lived in a large home at 162 Stanley Place, Hackensack, New Jersey. My aunts, Mae, Lydia, and Jessie went to school and worked; but they also took turns taking care of me when my grandmother, who was a registered nurse, went to work. I certainly thought one of those familiar faces would be coming through that door bringing me another bottle. One of them had always been reliable to spoil me like that.

Boy, I was wrong. "GIRL, I'M GOING TO FIX YOU NOW!" was this shout from this giant of a man marching in only to pick me up, hold me on one arm and spank my butt with his other hand like I was a drum. After the spanking, he forcefully put me back in the crib on my butt and marched out. I pulled myself up and stood in the crib crying and trying to figure out – "What the H _ _ _ just happened and why?!"

At about three years old, I recognized that man was Uncle Art marching furiously into the room, shouting and scaring me. (He had been in the Army and served his time in the Pacific. When I came along, he was a Colonel in the National Guard.)

Aunt Oquaritta and Uncle Art

The only thing he understood was that EVERYONE needed to follow "THE RULES". He was louder than the passenger train that cuts through our middle-class neighborhood every 15 to 20 minutes. The same tracks would have long freight trains frequently on weekends. The whistle of the horn was loud and the way the train shook our home required us to ignore the shaking if we wanted to keep our sanity.

Uncle Art was married to my mother's sister Oquaritta, and as I grew up, I believed they were perfect for each other. They could have formed their own military of very smart, talented, and mean people. They should have gone to OZ for hearts, but never did.

I guess I must have figured out that the spanking had something to do with the milk/soda can I had thrown out of my crib. This punishment made it hard to want any kind of bottle ever again. But I guess that was his point. To please everyone else, I started drinking under duress from a cup. Uncle Art's swift actions got me off the bottle. But it also made me fearful of him. He found time to spank me more often than I care to remember. Other cousins have confirmed he spanked them, too. Always with his hand, not a belt.

All this began in my grandparents' bedroom — Daddy and Mama White — sometime between 1948 and 1951. I like to remember this home I grew up in. A Google search shows that it still is a corner house. However, the large tree in the front yard and the hedge surrounding the perimeter are no longer there. The wrap-around porch wasn't enclosed back then.

When I lived there, one could readily see the seashell- shaped metal lawn furniture. There always were always two chairs against the wall closer to the front door on the porch. These chairs were for Mama White and Daddy White to sit in during the evening or one for Mama White to sit in with a basket of string beans ready for snapping on the other chair. At the end of the porch was the mint green metal swing. If you chose to go in the

162 Stanley Place, Hackensack, New Jersey

front door or back door, you would hear the music coming from the mechanism attached to the doors. Whenever you opened the doors "Twinkle, twinkle little star, how I wonder what you are?" was the familiar tune heard every day.

When coming through the front door, there was a full- length mirror in the front room. Below the mirror were the couch and the coffee table that I would eventually hit my head on. To your left was the large television near the stairs leading up to the second floor. The only bathroom and three bedrooms were on the second floor. There were two large bedrooms on the third floor.

When I was seven years old, I slept with my grandmother. When I was nine, I was allowed to sleep in the front bedroom on the third floor. However, I always wanted to sleep in the bedroom in the basement across from the huge coal stove. I was never allowed to sleep in the basement bedroom by myself. It was quiet down there. A space without noise. A place where one could relax without needing to be ready to obey the rules or adult requests of the moment.

On the day I gave up my bottle, the bedroom was filled with sunlight. There was a large round mirror on the wall right behind my crib. I spent a lot of time looking in it and making faces at myself. There were windows on one side of the room and a big bed just behind the door as you came into the room. Most of the time that bedroom door was closed, but I could hear the music from the record player filter into the room. Sometimes someone would sit down and play the organ.

There were sliding wood doors that separated the dining room from the front room. In the dining room was a large dining room table for eight. I would one day play under that dining table, and only once did I run under it to avoid a spanking from my grandmother.

There used to be a fireplace in the dining room, but it had been closed because of the draft, and because sometimes the birds would enter the home through it.

Next to the fireplace was a window in the wall with the kitchen on the other side so that food could be passed from the kitchen into the dining room. Leading to the corner was the Parakeets' (Jack and Jill) cage hanging from the ceiling, and a medium fish tank for the Guppies. A small organ with a record player stood in one corner of this room. The China cabinet was in the dining room, too. On the first floor were the kitchen and the pantry. The house had white shingles and a forest green trim. Our family appreciated our home, even though it would shake every time the train ran throughout the day.

As I began this personal tale, I asked my Aunt Jessie about my reaction to an empty bottle. She said, "Yes, you were great at throwing the bottles when they were empty. Mama White fixed a soda can so you could drink the formula from it."

While talking with Aunt Jesse, I recalled that event even better. She confirmed that she was the one who came and comforted me as I stood crying in the crib that day. Maybe that was the beginning of bonding with Aunt Jessie. I always felt she cared for me and my welfare.

I don't know how long I was in that crib, but I do remember the sounds I heard more often than people talking; it was the music and singing from the record player on the first floor. My grandfather, an ordained minister, played a lot of gospel records all day and into the night. Mahalia Jackson, George Beverly Shea, and Tennessee Ernie Ford songs filtered up to the second floor into the bedroom and into my ears and into my consciousness – thus continued the imprinting[1]. Before I knew the meaning of the words from these songs, they were cemented into my brain. Can you imagine what would happen if you heard day in and day out the lyrics to "If I Can Help Somebody"? The lyrics, like water drops upon my head, are as follows:

First Verse:

If I can help somebody, as I pass along
If I can cheer somebody, with a word or song
If I can show somebody, that he's traveling wrong
Then my living shall not be in vain

(Chorus)
My living shall not be in vain
Then my living shall not be in vain
If I can help somebody, as I pass along
Then my living shall not be in vain
Second Verse:
If I can do my duty, as a good man ought
If I can bring back beauty, to a world up wrought
If I can spread love's message, as the Master taught
Then my living shall not be in vain

These lyrics were my grandfather's favorite recordings. He played the record player continuously and loud. When I got older, I remember my grandmother's voice – "John, you know you need to turn that music down. It's too loud." He would always turn the music up, not down. When he left the house, Mama would turn the record player down or off.

Certainly, there were other songs that imprinted my heart growing up. Let me share a few of those songs with the lessons I attribute to them.

"*I'm A Little Tea Pot*" — Service to others...

"*The Bear Went Over the Mountain*" – Always move forward to conquer another goal...

"*Row, Row, Row Your Boat*" — Always moving forward... the struggle is worth it.

I knew I was an observer growing up. Daddy, Mother Dear, and Mama made sure that our household

Daddy, Mother Dear, and Mama
in the backyard in Hackensack.

was a Dictatorship, not a Democracy. "Children are to be seen and not heard." "Stay out of grown folks' business." "Don't you have some work to do?" "Go out and play, but don't leave the front yard. Don't leave the backyard." I began talking at three years old but did not talk much. I listened and observed more.

There were other means of imprinting the soul. There were the household chores. I was two or almost three when I learned how to sweep down the carpeted stairs. I was so small that both of my hands were needed to control the whisk broom. By five years old, I knew how to polish the banister railing, and also how to dust the knick-knacks in front of the stained-glass window on the landing going up to the second floor. Sometimes I was allowed to answer the telephone and ask who it was. This was to teach me telephone etiquette.

Here I am answering the telephone.

"Mama, Aunt Oquaritta is on the phone."

"Mama, is this okay? I can't get the dirt right here under the arm of this piece."

"It's okay. You did real good. You are a big girl now. It's time to get ready for bed and say your prayers."

Putting on my pink pajamas with the writing on the front — "You're a Sleepy Head," I then washed my face and brushed my teeth. I was not ever eager to say my prayers.

"Now I lay me down to sleep. I pray the Lord my soul to keep. If I should die before I wake, I pray the Lord my soul to take. I'll go to sleep now, Mama."

"Let me tuck you in. You stay under these covers until morning, or you might catch a cold. You understand?"

"Yes, Mama. Oh, let me go pee, and I'll be right back." "Thanks, *Mama, for tucking me in. I will set the table when I get up in the morning."*

"Don't worry about that, child. Just get yourself a good night's sleep."

I always thought it was a miracle to wake up in the morning.

Daddy White had my cousin, Lamont, and me up at dawn to work in the garden even before I was old enough to go to school. I still remember his instructions: "...Girl, remember, three seeds per hole in this dirt."

"Look, Daddy, I put three seeds in each of the holes. Is that okay?"

"Yes, that's just right. We're going to grow a lot of corn." My family believed reading was important. The first book, other than the Bible — King James Version — was John Bunyan's Pilgrim's Progress. My grandfather required an oral book review on what I gleaned from my reading. The concern of hurting yourself while helping another was never discussed. *"We are soldiers in the Army. We have to fight although we have to cry. We have to hold up the bloodstained banner. We have to hold it up until we die."*

It wasn't until I got to high school that I read Ayn Rand's *The Art of Selfishness*. Thank Goodness! This book, among others like Ibsen's *Doll House*, certainly contributed to greater conflicts with my Soul's original imprinting. Too many books, like *The Taming of the Shrew*, and other Shakespeare-type stories had made me believe the male is always right, and a woman should know her place.

From the moment I was born in Hackensack Hospital, Hackensack, New Jersey, my Soul has been imprinted in ways that make me who I am. Hackensack was very much a "Mayberry, USA," except there were Negros, Puerto Ricans, Jews, Cubans, and a few Asians, but mostly White folks. The railroad track separated the White folks from the rest of us, so people would come out on their porches whenever a White person was seen walking the sidewalks. They needed to know if the person was lost or who they had come to see.

I was almost nine before the trains' gatekeeper's hut was replaced by a mechanical gate. It was about that time when a supermarket was built up the street from my grandparent's home.

Many times, food was purchased from folks selling out of their trucks, or when Mama shopped for food at the market downtown.

As with buildings, once the foundation is laid, the building is built upon it. Consequently, when I re-examine "Me," I find that the foundation is as solid as it ever was. No termites here, only resolve to construct a firm foundation that could hold me up as long as I live. My mantra was formulated early in my life: "Help me to know what to say, and how to say it. Help me to know what to do, and know how to do it, and have the wisdom and ability to follow through."

There's a lot of history between the ages of 5 to 73. But I'm not ready to go into all of that. After all, this is a short story to give insight into why I am the way I am. It's not a biography of my life to date. It's important to know the foundation is basically the same. This foundation helped me when I went to school and observed that when I undid my braids, my hair stuck out, while my friends' (White girls) hair fell to their shoulders. I would imitate them by shaking my head as they did, but my hair did not flow around my face and neck like theirs did. In kindergarten, I learned that my skin looked different than most of the other children's skin in the class.

"But I want Billy to be my boyfriend."

Alice, blond and blue-eyed patiently explained, "No, Billy can't be your boyfriend. Don't you see he's White and you are a Negro."

"I'm a girl. I'm not a Negro."

"Yes, you are! You're a Negro. You're a Negro."

Consequently, I understood how going to a predominately White school may seriously hinder positive African-American Imprinting. Family still provided the love that I needed as a child. It provided the "You're okay" that helps a Black girl become a Black Woman. Still, words were said that created some conflicts in my head: "Come get your hair pressed, so you can look pretty." I thought I was pretty because I had hair that liked to stand up and be noticed. My aunts and grandmother were constantly telling me to not unbraid my hair when I got to school. But, when my hair was loose and standing out and about my head, I thought it was just as nice as the White girls' hair.

It was clear growing up that my family didn't have the money to go to the Yacht Club or the horse stable to ride horses for the weekend. We had love. We had time for each other. We had time to joke and make each other smile. We had unconditional love for each other...well, most of the time.

My grandparents stressed the importance of an education. When I was 5 years old, my grandfather placed me upon two phone books at the dining room table to learn to write my ABCs in cursive. In kindergarten, I learned how to print, but at home, I learned how to write. My grandparents, aunts, and uncles took the time to give us children a foundation to build upon as we became adults.

Smoking, drinking, and dancing were frowned upon in my grandparents' home, but flip that coin and you would see all three activities at their grown children's homes. So, I learned that there are places and times some things are acceptable, and then, there are times and places they are not. This conflicting Imprinting took time to reassess and accept as I got older.

Wearing a Sunday church hat and gloves was important, but not as important as reading and knowing the Bible. Attending the Christian school taught me that many Christian children behave in many different ways ... not always Angelic.

In an odd way, I learned that Black is not always black, and White is not always white. I encountered people like Larry Elder and Clarence Thomas who look African- American but don't appreciate our history. There are people like activist Tim Wise who look and are White but understand how important it is to be a good "human being."

Learning to observe and know people and situations helped me stay alive ... and be happy. Early on, I realized some of the people who shouted how "Black and Proud" they were, were authentic oreo cookies. They said they were all Black, but careful observation showed them to be Black on the outside with serious Right-wing White views on the inside.

Through books, studies and observations, I built upon my foundation. I learned to say, "Thank God for the abolitionists." I thank God for the "Good People." They come from all countries and cultures and should not be judged before they prove who they are. These are the people who are real Mensch, people who had also been imprinted with the notion of helping others. I figure they, too, had some good imprinting while growing up.

Sometimes, I meet some dark Souls who must not have had any of the positive imprinting I received. My Soul's light stays on because of the strong imprinting I had as a baby, child, and adult. The desire to help others remains, but in a more measured way. There are social issues that are important to me. I do my part in helping bring awareness, and I strive to correct some of these issues. "No man is an island." I realize that it is important to stand up for "Black Lives Matter". It's important to fight to change the gun laws. It is important to help fix global warming. The list is long on what I desire to be involved in. Now, it's not just for others, it's for me. I stay engaged in the issues because I want this Big Blue Marble of a planet to be a great place to live.

I am aware of the need to help myself. I am aware of the love and devotion I have for family, especially my husband and my son. Others follow as individuals I am blessed to know as family and friends. But now I know that if one does not help "Self", then truly, "Your living is in vain."

I suggest you should know what has and is imprinting *your* Soul. Be thoughtful and careful as you imprint your children's Souls and/or others you influence. Be mindful of what you say. Be mindful of what you do. I think this should be your duty as a Soulful Being.

LOOKING BACK...

...over the years, I realize that those experiences and memories developed me into who I am today. Those "Moments-in-Time" make it possible for me to see the future with grand possibilities ... even in today's Covid-infected World. I am one who keeps "Hope" alive.

About the Author: Zola Salena-Hawkins
Author / Photographer / Certified Tai Chi Instructor

Zola Salena-Hawkins has always been an individual who studied people, places, and things. She started writing non-fiction as a teenager, striving to be something of a "Dr. Gray" as she analyzed various members of her family. Unfortunately, that journal was removed from its hiding place presumably by her grandparents. (They never mentioned it, she never mentioned it.) Graduate of Hackensack High School, Hackensack, New Jersey and Cal State University, Dominguez Hills, CA.; there were numerous papers, reports, and treatises on various subjects: Social Studies, Religion and History. Working at Jacoby & Meyers opened her eyes to numerous legal subjects. Her previous education and work experience allowed her to assist in writing declarations and trial briefs. Finally, at the Department of Justice she had opportunities to make suggestions for several projects, including a manual on how to process the Hague International Child Abduction Cases.

In 1980 she illustrated the cover to "Up the Job Market: Finding Your Way...A Sociology Workbook on Jobs" by Jeanne Curran and Carol Telesky, Department of Sociology, California State University, Dominguez Hills. In the '80's she had one of her poems published in "African American Heritage Magazine", Published by Dellco Publishing Company in Inglewood, CA. During most of the time she worked in the law offices, she took a hiatus from drawing, sculpture, modeling, photography and writing. She is currently illustrating and photographing covers for author Odie Hawkins; and has returned to some of her previous endeavors. Zola is a Certified Tai Chi Instructor and is currently studying to be a Certified Personal Trainer.

Odie Hawkins, her husband, has helped her open up her creative and imaginative mindset. She enjoys writing political satire and returning to what makes people "tick". Consequently, we have this first piece entitled "Imprinting My Soul".

linkedin.com/in/zola- salena-hawkins-41794755/
flickr.com/photos/32886903@N02

FIVE

WATTS RAISED

Ron L. Dowell

1960's

RON L. DOWELL is the author of Watts UpRise, *a poetry collection released by World Stage Press in July 2022. Watts UpRise is a very public love letter to Watts, Los Angeles. The collection honors its most notable artistic landmark, the Watts Towers, and its creator, Sabato Rodia. The Towers epitomize the beauty, strength, and resiliency of the city and its inhabitants and serve as a reminder that beautiful things we must keep heart-close and love. Here, Ron tells his story.*

Had Martin Luther King Jr. Hospital been built on July 7, 1951, to birth their firstborn, Mom and Dad could've traveled two instead of the ten miles it took to traverse Alameda Street to Big G Hospital from the Jordan Downs Public Housing Projects. Initially built in the 1940s as housing for workers during World War II, Jordan Downs's 700 drab amber units were converted to public housing in the 1950s.

The trek to Big G was always bumpy, and instead of trees, Alameda was lined with the clang of industrial factories and junk yards. Whether we were at home listening to AM radio from the bread loaf-sized dark brown radio or in one of Dad's brand-new second-hand hooptees, there was one constant: Little Willie John's record "Fever." *You never know how much I love ya/Never know how much I care/When you put your arms around me/I get a feelin' that's so hard to bear/You give me fever.* ("Little Willie John - Fever

Lyrics - SONGLYRICS.com")

Richard was born in May 1952. However, King wasn't completed until 1971, fifteen years after we moved into Palm Lane Public Housing and six years after the so-called 1965 "Watts Riot," which burned most of the commercial 103rd Street and pointed to the fact that "inner city" residents of Watts had inadequate access to healthcare facilities. Still, before King, most of Mom's pre- and postnatal appointments were also at Big G, as were the slew of checkups and vaccinations for my brother and me. Any in-between sickness meant we scrambled into one of Dad's project cars and headed north. We never had a new car, but we had a series of used cars that Dad always seemed to work on, like the four-door lime green 55 Chevy my mom drove. He ensured mom's car was drivable enough to get her to work, markets, and our grandparent's urban farmhouse across the street from us. Mom, Richard, and I headed west on 120th Street in her Chevy one day. Richard was upfront as I hung over the seat, thumping his head with a thumb and pointer finger. We all saw Dad driving in the opposite direction in his Ford Deluxe with another woman riding shotgun sidled up close to him, grinning like a Cheshire cat. Mom's eyes went cold, flinty. I said, "Is that—?"

She said, "SIT DOWN AND SHUT UP."

Excerpt from Watts UpRise:

Give Us This Day
This was 1963, and by the time the Iron Trinity trickled
to him, his mechanical skills weren't enough
to keep rolling what later became "collectibles."
A sleek, low profile '49 Chevy Fleetline
with bulging rear fenders, the turd-brown
'52 Chevy Styleline—the shoebox '51 Ford Deluxe
all with dings like bullets, rusting doglegs
wheel wells, and weak floorboards...

As a kid, I always enjoyed reading D.C. comics, Mad

Magazines, and the Compton Encyclopedias my mother purchased from the white-haired White man door-to-door salesman for Richard and me. Every year, he'd bring a book to add to our collection.

My parents migrated from Bonham, Texas. My mom, aunt, grandmother, and grandfather stopped in Arizona long enough for my mom to graduate from Tucson High School in 1947, the same year that Jack Robinson opened the baseball floodgates to Black people and other POC. Every non-white baseball player earning millions to play baseball in the major leagues is indebted to Jackie Robinson.

Excerpt from Watts UpRise:

A 1947 Negro Conversation

But Robinson plays baseball better'n anyone.
Fleetwood Walker played major
sixty years before Jack
Won't happen
too much prejudice
rope and gun
But Robinson plays great.
Negro's league homespun
better'n most whites, Doby, Paige,
he's no gimcrack.
But Robinson plays baseball better'n anyone,
faster than wind, hits fastballs to the sun.
It's true. I looked it up in the almanac.
Won't happen
too much prejudice
rope and gun
Like Negro women on silver screens,
never outdone castaway maid
nanny carries baby piggyback.
But Robinson plays baseball better'n anyone.

Baseball was huge for Blacks once Robinson and others took

the field. I started playing at about nine at Gopher Hole Stadium in Palm Lane. Over two hundred households lived in a nexus of L.A. County Housing Authority single-story, roach-infested, flat-roofed fourplex apartments with quarter-inch sheetrock walls splayed across 26 acres, a county strip between Watts and the city of Compton: a sort of neutral zone between disparate communities, like an O ring used to seal opposing surfaces against high pressure. Since our family's unit was on the left-field foul line, baseballs often crashed into our windows, front door, and roof. I had to learn to either hate or love baseball. With a transistor radio under my pillow, I chose love and regularly listened to Vin Scully broadcast Dodgers games. When Frank Howard hit a homer against

Palm Lane Public Housing

the Giants, he'd say, "...it's a high drive to deep left field. Back goes Alou, way back, to the wall...it's gone!"

Scully painted word pictures of the game, as few were telecast on our black and white television. Baseball comes easy if you play from sun up to sun down all year round. Gerald Campbell, brothers Glen and Gerald Adams, Jojo Lee, and I did that until Mom hollered from our concrete porch, "Ronnie, it's time to eat—get in here." Reluctantly, I'd acquiesce.

✳ ✳ ✳ ✳ ✳

1965 left a hole in my baseball trophy collection. My teams won trophies in 1963, 64, 66, and 67. Unfortunately, the Watts Rebellion ended our 1965 season prematurely. Police ignited the uprising when they bashed in a drunken Marquette Frye's Black head in skin-color-segregated L.A. Thirty-four people died, and ambulances transported hundreds more to emergency rooms miles away. Playgrounds closed; trash piled up when sanitation workers refused to pick it up, and thousands of National Guard troops were added to the police already in Watts.

Excerpt from Watts UpRise:

Anger Management in a Time of COVID-19 Pandemic and Riotous Grief

First, understand what you call "a riot,"
was the Watts rebellion ending our 1965
Little League season. No last-inning strikeout
but choking smoke, thick burning rubber.

No walk-off home run, but smoldering wood.
No game-winning catch, but chemicals
Scorching our throats, chest, lungs,
interrupting me & Gerald's
sunrise to sundown baseball passion on
Gopher Hole Stadium, redlined with public dollars.
No—...

Baseball can be instructive as success and failure are based on statistics. I learned to calculate batting averages "by dividing the number of hits by the number of at-bats. I learned the value of team play and how to rely on others and be responsible for my role. Today, players make goo gobs by getting one hit in every three at-bats.

Later, I taught my three children how to play and often coached their teams. My oldest son Aaron played for Gerald Pickens, also known as Coach G, and dedicated himself to maintaining baseball play in Compton for over forty years. My daughter, Kamilah, played softball in Wilmington, as there was little to no such play in Compton at the time. She traveled to tournaments all over the state. I still recall an impossible shoestring catch she made in a game. Ahmad was good at everything from soccer to basketball. He sometimes thought it hard to accept that he could achieve anything he set his mind to. They are all college grads, two with master's degrees. When you include their mother's Master's, whom I was separated from before we divorced, and my two, there are as many postgraduate degrees as Dowell's.

Excerpt from Watts UpRise:

Aaron Lee

We talked through your mother's stretch marks
months after the seed was planted.
Your bubbly gurgle, a kick to my ear
signaled you were listening.
Your black-and-white sonogram-self
turned, winked, & said
I'm on my way, world.
My eldest son, the middle
of three, once you loved
the green skull cap, red
propeller on top, spinning.
You loved life & life loved
you back—the wonder of insects,
the warmth of a tub bath—
rain pounding our roof, windows...

✷ ✷ ✷ ✷ ✷

I thank Mom for helping me learn to read. My dad claimed he had a third-grade education, but one day, when I was in my early twenties, I saw him lying on our plastic-covered sofa, leafing through an upside-down newspaper. It hit me so hard, like a lightning bolt, that Dad could not read. Then, I understood why mom always paid the bills, managed the family business, and assembled toys for Mattel Toymakers. Dad swept out boxcars for Pacific Fruit Express and always did manual labor. He mowed lawns to support his family for a living after PFE laid him off before retirement. Consistent, he rose early, left for work daily, and presented a dynamic role model for me.

I turned 14 just before the Watts Uprising. I'd tasted cheap wines like White Port and Silver Satin with bitter lemon a year or two earlier. Unlike with some of my homies, drinking was nothing serious in early adolescence, just something to do on the way to house parties. The wine, however, did ease my fear of asking girls to dance, as I did not like rejection. Nor did I regularly practice dance steps like I practiced baseball.

Once, I jumped in line to dance with Betty since she'd hold me tight and grind her body against mine as Garnet Mimms's *Cry Baby* played. Betty knew what she was doing since we were pubescent, and I wanted to screw anything moving. She only teased me, dangling sex like a puppet master. She never gave me any, but she did become pregnant while we were still in junior high school. I was shy and ignorant of the ways of women.

After the riot, our streets flooded with all sorts of drugs: Lilly Pharmaceutical bullet-head F40s, Quaaludes, phencyclidine, and everything from acid to cocaine to weed to heroin were readily available to me and affordable. In late summer 1966, I swallowed the first two red devils found wrapped in foil near the curb at our newly purchased home, a Willie McCovey homerun from King Hospital. Within minutes, the soothing euphoria hit my body and annexed my brain. It was oxymoronic to believe I could be on top of everything under the influence of barbiturates and alcohol. Earlier that year, the county housing authority evicted us from Palm Lane with hundreds of other households to make way for the Dr. Martin Luther King Jr. Hospital. Soon after, I bought my first joint from Booker at Centennial High School. My drug experimentation increased inversely to my baseball play and school grades; by 1967, I had stopped playing the game. Thus grew my addiction beast and subsequent series of escalating petty criminal activities to feed it.

★ ★ ★ ★ ★

Looking back, I now understand what Steve Biko meant when he said, "The most potent weapon of the oppressor is the mind of the oppressed." Over the years, another of his quotes has rung true for me: "Black man, you are on your own." We rarely saw or interacted with white people in Watts except for a few store merchants, door-to-door salesmen, teachers, and, of course, police. Restrictive housing covenants installed in the mid-twentieth century were in full effect during the 1950s and 60s.

A druggie's behavior is predictable. Awaken, crave, plot, execute, shoot up/snort/spike/swallow, skin-pop/smoke (or whatever your administration mode)/sleep/repeat. Although drug use gave me the false courage to talk to Mysteree, my first real girlfriend and my drug use simultaneously planted the seeds of our relationship failure. Fortunately, I was too damn scared to spike a needle even though I snorted boy [heroin] and girl [cocaine] a couple of times. For several years, my life spiraled out of control thanks to any pills or drinks handed to me. One day I ditched high school, and my best friend Glen set me up with his cousin Yolanda for my first shot of pussy. A couple of years younger than me, Yolanda was a pro at sex with a couple of children to show for it. She was petite, had short-pressed hair, dark skin, nice thick lips, and nearly sucked the tongue out of my mouth. She blew my fuckin' mind in my twin bed while my parents were at work. Little Willie John blasted into my mind: *You give me fever/When you kiss me/Fever when you hold me tight/Fever in the mornin'/Fever all through the night.*

Afterward, for a repeat, I chased Yolanda all over Imperial Courts Public Housing until I caught the claps. Once my shit started to drip and burn, Mom sent me to Dad, who, in turn, pointed me to the county health clinic for penicillin. Addicts take all kinds of risks and will fuck anyone any time, if not too high, and, consequently, are particularly vulnerable to STDs. We also tend to get lots of cuts and scrapes, like the shin gash I received while jacking up my car when buzzed. A drug-dependent person will do almost anything to get more, and I did. I'd steal anything to sell, even mom's blue-chip stamp books. She had to know but never said a word. Without a job, crime was the option to maintain drug habits, and I ran with others with the same problems.

We dope fiends never considered that our addiction-fueled crime sprees, purse snatching, car theft, follow-home robberies, burglary, and shoplifting were doomed to fail with our fogged-up brains. We never considered quitting drugs an option for those of us who survived those times, changing ingrained habits we never questioned. Sizing up crime opportunities is what we did, never considering that this behavior may have been part of a grander design aided and abetted by American apartheid.

I learned to shoplift from Cliff Winrow. We were the same age, but Cliff was a short kid who looked much younger than his age. At 13 or 14, he looked around nine or ten, even eight. To steal fishing equipment from Sears, he'd grab items and follow an adult out of the store in Compton as if he were their child. The scheme worked for baseball equipment or whatever he wanted. Using similar techniques, we would steal baseballs and mitts from Thrifty Drugstore. We'd use the ball until the rawhide covers fell off, tape them with duct tape, and continue playing with them. Eventually, the tape failed and revealed the twine underneath, which we unraveled and played stickball with the small rubber ball inside. Of course, after a couple of hits, the ball disappeared into a yard some distance away.

✴ ✴ ✴ ✴ ✴

Around 1970, within the tight grip of drug addiction, I was nineteen and loved music but was broke as hell was hot. I could never get the coveted gas station attendant or Sears floor salesperson job as Ralph McNeal had. I spent my time in the student lounge/cafeteria watching Tonk, Gin Rummy, and Spades card games or off the Compton College campus instead of classrooms. I could, however, steal. I would apply what I learned from Cliff.

At Sears, I leafed through the record album racks, carefully selecting Motown, jazz, and some rock and roll, like the Rolling Stones, Beatles, and Iron Butterfly, about 10 to 15 of my favorites. I was high and foolish and looked around but saw no off-duty police masquerading as floorwalkers. With booty under both arms, I wound my way behind an older Black couple. I smiled as we drew closer to the exit door and could see myself at home playing the Supremes', *Someday We'll Be Together*, or John Coltrane's, *My Favorite Things* on my small battery-operated record player.

The couple cleared the exit with me about 10 feet behind. I pushed a yard past the threshold of the exit door. "HOLD IT," said a man's baritone. My breath caught short when a hand horse collared me from behind. "You didn't pay for that," the plainclothes cop said.

"But...but," I managed to squeeze out. I dropped the albums and was hurried to a basement area in Sears. After the interrogation, I was whisked to the Compton PD jail.

Drug use took me to the most undesirable places, like the Big House. Located around 119th Street and Holmes, the Big House was a two-story wood-framed multi-unit building. Its many rooms might make it a good boarding house or halfway house today. Always dark and spooky, it's where I often copped pills from people whose faces I could never clearly see. In the dankness, I blinked rapidly, my heartbeat causing chest pain whenever I stepped inside the musty structure.

"What you need?" came a voice.

"A deuce," I said.

"One dollar," the voice said. I glimpsed what looked like a trench coat. I pushed the voice a dollar and received a tiny foil-wrapped packet. Often, the product was weak but true. I would never stand there and open the purchase, opting to leave and walk some distance away from the Big House.

We are born with all we'll ever need, yet for some reason, we believe that adding foreign substances to the mix will somehow improve God's perfection. I drank the Kool-Aid by the gallon. It's no different today, albeit the drugs are much more powerful. Most of us can't afford refined products and often rely on some stepped-on concoction mixed by a mis-educated alchemist who failed chemistry. For Black people, the consequences of our drug use are dire since we don't have the safety nets to resurrect from the damage to body, mind, and soul. As it is, we suffer the most undesirable health outcomes, high blood pressure, sugar diabetes, and heart disease, receive the worst self-care information, if any at all, attend the worst schools, and continue to suffer from American segregation and systemic racism ingrained like knots in hardwood. Since we live with Latinos in ethnic segregation, our drug use and concomitant crime mean that our neighbors are the primary victims or prey.

Even as marijuana becomes more decriminalized across the nation, many Blacks, particularly men, serve prison time for cannabis-related offenses. For you, the reader, to be forewarned is to be forearmed. We live in the good ol' USA, the United States of Addiction, under a United States Constitution that considers us three-fifths human.

✳ ✳ ✳ ✳ ✳

My secondary schooling was not the best, and I was not always the best student, especially after elementary school, where, with loving help from Mom, at least I learned to read. School, particularly for Black boys, sucked. Few of us seemed encouraged to take education seriously, use the library, or seek anything other than a manual labor "job."

I'm proud that despite my D GPA out of Centennial High in Compton in 1969, I bore migraines and turned everything around during my second stint at Compton College from 1971 to 73. I'm okay with being the first several-time college graduate in my family. I'm okay coming of age with Black Panther and Black Muslim influence. I'm good with helping to mitigate the erasure of a Black male's experience growing up in South Central Los Angeles.

However, I was still drug dependent in my early twenties when I took drawing classes at Compton College. By then, I worked as a community worker for the L.A. County Department of Mental Health. It is said that God works in mysterious ways. True that.

At first, the staff resented ten trainees from Operation T.R.A.I.N. The federal program was intended to bridge the service gap between the center and the Compton/Watts community. Community members had little trust or confidence in what mental health offered, and our task was to share and, sometimes, deliver basic counseling and referral services.

My best friend David Edmond and I were the youngest among trainees selected for the program at 20 and 19, respectively. We found ourselves officed at facing wood desks in the back of the lunchroom kitchen area. I thank God David never used drugs and was a rampart against some of my craziness, like when I'd drive the white county station wagon with the county logo into Nickerson Gardens to buy pills. Although he would side-eye me, neither my street pharmacist nor I cared about the county emblem on the station wagon doors.

Sechon and David Edmond

Co-workers offered to buy my drawings. They were sympathetic and empathetic toward me as the low-man-on-the-totem-pole in an otherwise college degree and professional setting. David and I later gravitated toward a public health nurse at Southeast Mental Health named Sechon, who was intensely interested in all things uplifting, spiritual, and artistic. Although he had a first name, he preferred being called by his surname, and everyone obliged. Sechon's drug expertise was known nationwide. As such, he was brought in to install alcohol and other drug programs in the center, as the other social workers, psychiatrists, and technicians knew little beyond their struggles with substances. He always said, "If you don't have a program, there's always someone to give you one." Sechon demanded that David and I relocate from the kitchen and be assigned to him. The head psychiatrist, Dr. Boyd, acquiesced. That move began the drug recovery service at Southeast Mental Health Center.

Under Sechon's mentorship, I learned to silversmith Native American jewelry since it was far less expensive to make than buy. He'd add, "Ronnie, your way of thinking has gotten you to where you are. Sometimes, we might need others to think for us to move forward." My chest tightened when he said these things to me, but I understand when I think about how hard it was to give up my inclination to plot and steal. "What you do speaks much louder than anything you say," was another saying that pissed me off.

When I offered flimsy excuses for backsliding, he'd hold up the palm of his hand to represent a reflective mirror of my attempts to bullshit the master prophet. He taught me the basics of photography and led me to appreciate travel. Years later, I started a videography business because people seemed willing to pay me for what I would otherwise do for free. I love taking pictures and have traveled to Canada, Cuba, England, France, Thailand, Malaysia, South Korea, South Africa, Central and South America. Sechon became my third parent and did what the other two could not: give tough love and demonstrate selflessness. For a selfish bastard like me, it worked.

Quitting barbiturates is dangerous, and death can and does occur for some dope fiends. Despite excessive sweating, headaches, heart palpitations, and hyperventilating episodes, by 1971, I cleaned up my drug dependence with love and support from Sechon and David, internal fortitude, and great withdrawal difficulty. I eased off with the help of Stelazine, a psychotropic prescribed by Dr. Woods, the workplace psychiatrist known for treating celebrities. The intense counseling sometimes felt like an exorcism.

Sechon was good at his craft and was noticed. He accepted a promotional offer to spread his expertise beyond the mental health center to the entire region. He took David and me with him. I later found myself working as an alcohol and other drug program planner for what the county called the Southeast Healthcare Region (Watts, Compton, South Central). My job was to write the county plan for "treatment services." I had to research to write the alcohol proposal component and convince the head office to fund local recovery programs. Another public health nurse, Fay Wilson, was our liaison to the Office of Alcoholism and Alcohol Abuse (OAAA). David had the same task on the drug side as then alcohol was not considered a drug inexplicably. Later, David and I were promoted to the head offices, me to OAAA, and he to DAPO (Drug Abuse Program Office) to audit contract programs.

The Southeast Region job enabled me to travel all over L.A. County. Sechon was my plan's editor and often red-inked my drafts like he once did hospital patient charts. As painful as this process was, I now see how it prepared me to become a journalist, poet, and story writer later. Most of all, I learned how to accept criticism and rejection.

It was clear that the area with the most drug-related problems was the Southeast Healthcare Region. It soon became apparent that the Board of Supervisors and county bureaucrats would divvy the money uniformly throughout the county no matter how much data I presented or how persuasively or creatively I wrote the plan. In other words, areas with fewer negative impacts from drug use received the same money as the Southeast Region, sometimes more. Often, programs receive "sole source" contracts at the behest of a board member, resulting from political connections and influence. That preference mechanism subverted competitive bidding.

However, even though I didn't see it then, those years of writing service plans were my best introduction to creative writing. My drug-addled history honed my mission to dissuade others from the trap of alcohol and other drug use and psychological enslavement. I have learned to love myself more and understand that I cannot love others until I do. I share this reveal sanctimoniously in my poem.

Excerpt from Watts UpRise:

What I Learned from a Bell Pepper
I've turned inside out, stood unclothed
and often unlearned misteaching
by circles of the dead. To learn
we penetrate the skin, substrate,
don't settle for first impressions.
Listening is the first thing to do.
Too many times, I've heard you speak
and I wanted you to finish
so I could make my point. You'd ask
what I understood you to say
and I'd stand there scratching my head
disappeared like the Hoodoo

man rootwork. Feedback lets
others know we listened. Burdens
lift, community blossoms, shift
when we listen to each other
and if to you they won't listen...

I feel obligated to give back what I have received from Sechon, FayWilson, David Edmond, and so many others who, with their love and support, helped save me from myself. I overcame pills, cannabis, and alcohol addiction.

✳ ✳ ✳ ✳ ✳

I am likely the only sheriff employee who served time in its facilities before they hired me in 1991. That was late 1970, after a drug-fueled failed purse-snatching caper when I was sentenced to five weekends in jail. My journey began in Men's Central Jail during the initial arrest and first week of the sentence. Afterward, I reported to Biscailuz Center jail every Friday evening.

One Friday, since I couldn't figure out how to hollow out a shoe heel to conceal my crutch à la James Bond, I stuffed Eli Lilly, red devils, into the toe of my shoe with toilet paper. I shifted from foot to foot when the intake deputy squeezed the shoe toe and slammed the heel on the desk. The stumblers would have dislodged if he hit the heel first, revealing my stash. Since I couldn't get high, I spent my remaining weekends in jail reading the Autobiography of Malcolm X, which, weekend after weekend, was always available when I arrived. As I said before, drugs relax inhibitions, causing addicts to take foolish risks. I did a lot of stupid shit while under the influence.

By 1991, I was different, and the sheriff needed my financial skillset badly. Their employee, Patricia Jenkins, also held their feet to the fire so they would hire me. Pat's supply and warehouse unit ordered all medical supplies to support services for about 19-20 thousand prisoners spread across jails dispersed throughout L.A. County for the Medical Services unit.

Medical Services comprised about 500 doctors, dentists, nurses, pharmacists, radiology and laboratory techs, custodians, and admin staff. The jails are like mini-cities, and except for emergency treatment, births, and surgeries, Medical Services were the inmate's source of care.

My job was to deliver supplies to outlying locations, prepare the budget, and advocate for Medical Services, which the sheriffs called the "infirmary." Having worked twenty years in county healthcare, including public health and hospitals, I'd never heard this term used except on WWII television shows and movies. That was my first indication of how backward the sheriff's department was. I later found that the sheriffs didn't work well with the county's other 38 departments and were poorly liked. My office, along with Pat's down the hall, was located in the rear of Men's Central Jail, at the exit for inmates being bused to courts. The garbage bins were also just outside those perennially locked doors, and stink rushed our offices each time the doors opened. My delivery staff and I adapted to jailhouse funk, inmate fights, deputy coercion and force on inmates, the constant risk of catching TB, the clang of sallyport gates, plumbing leaks, constant lockdowns, and blackouts.

OJ Simpson was transported to court through the rear exit next to our offices. He spotted my secretary, Sharon, and made it his mission to crane his neck, smile, and wave at her each time he passed, which was often. Robert Downey, Jr. passed me in an orange jumpsuit at Biscailuz Center. Suge Knight was in the MCJ "keep-away" housing. I often passed relatives and old friends on the benches waiting for outpatient treatment services as I hunkered past the sallyport down the long wax-tiled hall to my office. Before transferring, I oversaw over 100 general services, pharmacy, medical technologist, and supply delivery personnel. I streamlined operations, installed performance indicators, and built teams. When I was promoted and transferred to the Records and Information Bureau, Medical Services transitioned from Men's Central Jail to the new Twin Towers, which had about 1500 personnel and a fivefold budget increase. I was part of the department's budget "Skunk Committee" and received commendations.

I communicated well with HQ's budget staff, who, before my arrival, had a disdain for medical services, as did most of the sheriff's department. For example, in a January 2000 memo under Lt. Richard Moak's signature, I penned a request to Pat Hawkins, Director of Fiscal Admin, where we asked for 1003 additional medical personnel to address inmate dialysis needs, the AIDS problem, and an uptick in mentally ill inmates. Our medical budget request exceeded the microscopic amount proposed by Fiscal Services, who did not know doodly-squat about patient care. By then, I had trained them to respect and accept medical budget needs. It helped our case that medical care was often the defendant in liability litigation like deputy uses of force. As medical personnel, we had to continually train sworn employees as their primary

Commendation received while leading the Property and Evidence unit

focus was kissing up for promotions, arresting and managing prisoners, and not servicing inmate medical requirements. It was common for sergeants, lieutenants, and captains to be assigned crucial Medical Services positions based solely on a relative who may have worked somewhere in a medical capacity. These people did not have a clue. The smarter ones, like Moak, signed the memos I handed him.

✸ ✸ ✸ ✸ ✸

Few people knew about the many hours I spent in libraries all over the Los Angeles area, learning new things and unlearning what needed to be improved in my life, workplace experiences, and art. I have often taken the road less traveled and chose paths, not knowing where they would lead. I will never give up serving my community, although I may have to change direction as I have so many times. I understood long before he did what Nipsey Hussle meant:

"...Dedication, hard work plus patience/The sum of all my sacrifice, I'm done waitin'/I'm done waitin', told you that I wasn't playin'/Now you hear what I been sayin'/dedication/It's dedication..."
("Nipsey Hussle - Dedication Lyrics | AZLyrics.com")

I added the element of informed risk and visited similar themes in my poetry piece.

Excerpt from Watts UpRise:

Breaking Point

For days, we've flown in tight formation
...I break rank and stiffen
will others follow? I'm never alone
without the constant song of our quarrel
without crumbs and worms from our hunters
without the comfort of our flock. What lies
outside us torments my familiar.
Songbirds that stray don't return to chirp
of separation's claim, what it means
to left turn, right, when flight direction points south.
I blink slowly on changing winds.
When my eyes reopen, I'm ocean-bound—

✷ ✷ ✷ ✷ ✷

I have an undergraduate business degree in accounting from California State University Dominguez Hills and passed the Uniform Certified Public Accountant Examination in the mid-80s. I needed two years of field auditing experience with a CPA firm to become certified. At the time, I worked as a program auditor in public health and wanted to mesh the best of public and non-governmental business approaches while preparing to leave public service for the private sector.

At first, I didn't know about accounting, which was hard. However, private-sector CPA firms viewed working for the public sector as a disadvantage during the 80s. There were also very few Black people in the profession that I could see when I attended events given by the accounting groups I joined. The first Black CPA I had ever seen, Andrew Smith, worked for Disneyland and taught courses at CSUDH, where I enrolled. By the time I took Smith's class, I had managed to survive Mr. Clawson's first-year accounting course. I believe Sechon convinced me to try accounting after receiving an undergraduate degree in anthropology in 1976. Clawson's class started with over 30 students and ended with eight. After bouts with migraine headaches, extensive library time and textbook reading and rereading, I was among the last ones standing and got a C grade.

I met in Clawson's office after the final exam. "Maybe you should pursue certified public accountancy," he suggested.

I nodded my head and said fuck you to him in my mind. My stomach clenched. After nearly killing my ass, this short fat white guy had his nerve. He had to be shitting me. I thanked him for allowing me to survive his course and left his office. I never wanted to see a spreadsheet again. A seed, however, was planted, which germinated more when I later saw Mr. Smith.

A private firm never employed me, and the one place within L.A. County public service that offered what I needed, the auditor-controller, never hired me even after two interviews at separate times. Negative self-talk crept into my mind with each Auditor-Controller's rejection as I am sure that few other county employees could match my accomplishments. Though I had a family to support, I was willing to take a demotion. It would be easy for me to attribute my Auditor-Controller experience to racism. I do.

However, I successfully experimented with private-sector business strategies while working for L.A. County Healthcare and later public safety (law enforcement), such as performance measurement, specific goal attainment, best practices, and team building. I developed a passion for process improvements using business solutions in the public sector. That passion, coupled with my love for writing, when, in 2010, I converted a master's degree thesis into a published book, *Compton4COPS: Community-Based Crime Fighting in Disadvantaged Racially and Ethnically Diverse Urban Communities.*

I was familiar with their operations since I worked in upper management for the Los Angeles County Sheriff's Department. LASD would never provide the kind or quality of service needed for Compton. They should have taken the time and tried to figure it out. Theirs is a one-size-fits-all antiquated service approach, a reactive slave patrol model, like a skeleton key used on an electric door.

Then as of now, I encourage Compton residents to take the city's public safety seriously and control it more. Minimally, I planned to start a community conversation about policing and public safety. The results are mixed. Police have controlled the narrative since their start as slave patrols. It is challenging for Compton residents to envision or consider other public safety options, significantly absent a clear view of what deputies do. When we do, we'll set the world on fire. Nevertheless, I thank former sheriff Leroy Baca for offering his employees an educational opportunity through CSULB.

Over a decade earlier, I started my tax preparation business, RonDowCo. Since *COPS* was self-published, I connected my poetry and fiction writing to another company and formed Deniggerlator Publishing. Like my earlier experiences with trying to transition to the private sector, the road would be difficult, and there are not a lot of Black faces in the literary world, especially males. Much of my personal experience and history is being erased, and few narratives tell my story, having been born and raised in Los Angeles.

On July 13, 2022, six days after my birthday, World Stage Press launched my poetry collection *Watts UpRise*. I feel

WattsUpRise
World Stage Press (2022)

incredibly fortunate to have run into Hiram Sims and the Community Literature Initiative (CLI) at the start of the COVID-19 pandemic, where I was part of the 2020 and 2021 cohorts. I had first taken poetry classes in the UCLA Extension Writers Program, but I sharpened the skills learned there in CLI. On Labor Day 2024, Running Wild Press's RIZE imprint released my short story collection, *Crooked out of Compton*.

Crooked out of Compton
RIZE (2024)

Around 2012, I stumbled across a means of serving my community and preserving some history: fiction writing and poetry. The UCLA Extension Writing Program taught me how to write creatively. I met mentors as a 2018 PEN America Emerging Voices Fellow, such as authors Tananarive Due and Douglas Manuel. My association with UCLA professors Lou Matthews, Colette Sartor, Paul Mandelbaum, Laurel Ann Bogen, and Suzanne Lummis has enabled me to write the abovementioned books.

I can't exclude my workshop groups: AC Bilbrew Writers Workshop, The Saturday Morning Literary Workshop, and Tertulia Literary Salon. Those groups give me a platform and invaluable feedback.

Once I retired from L.A. County in 2008, I continued to serve my community by working with several nonprofits that work with young people: Compton Baseball Academy Teams (CBATs), Teen Intervention Program (TIP), and Sports Spectacular.

My business is my writing; writing is my business, literally and figuratively. I combined both passions and wrote *Watts UpRise* and *Crooked out of Compton*. Having retired from L.A. County after 40 years as a public servant, half in healthcare and half in public safety (law enforcement), I'll always serve the public. What else do I know? I feel obligated to give back to my community, particularly the Watts and Compton areas where I grew up. I do for others what many have done for me.

I'm excited about an opportunity to connect gritty stories showing how people find hope and joy in lives where basic needs must be met. My poetry and stories discuss a suite of sociopolitical realities in an honest, innovative way—a way that challenges stereotypes and humanizes people.

I'm proud that *Watts UpRise* was a Press 53 finalist, that my poem "Compton, an energy-fueled dark star," is a Pushcart Prize nominee, and that World Stage Press liked the collection enough to publish it. I'm pleased that *Crooked Out of Compton* was a semi-finalist in the Chestnut Review Stubborn Artists Contest and a finalist for the Black Lawrence Press 2020 Big Moose Prize. My short story "Don't Worry" was a finalist in the 2021 Prime Number Magazine Award for Short Fiction. "Bruised" is a Tulip Tree Merit Prize winner.

Mention "California," and most people think of sun-kissed beaches, star-studded glamour, Hollywood success, or Silicon Valley. Mention Watts, and most think of so-called "Riots." "Compton" makes some folks think of gangs, gangsta rap, and crime. However, my art expands the narrative to include stories that reveal a different facet of the South [Central] Los Angeles community and its inhabitants.

I have taken folks from out of state to Compton. They always want to visit the "action." We might visit Patria Coffee, Angeles Abby, or New Earth Health Foods. Next, they ask, "When do we get to Compton?" We pass the King Memorial near Compton's city hall on our way to the Watts Towers. When they inevitably want the photo, I say, "We've been in Compton all along."

The Watts Towers are folk art/assemblage, a collection of seventeen sculptures built by Simon Rodia over 34 years. I show visitors my old home, Building #33, in Jordan Downs Public Housing, the resurrected Dr. MLK Jr. General Hospital and Big County General Hospital, over twenty miles away. That's where mom had to endure labor pains and the extended time to make that journey, as "Big G" was the only emergency hospital around. A luta continua.

Excerpt from Watts UpRise:

Watts UpRise
after Sabato "Simon" Rodia, "I'm gonna do something"

I'm gonna do something, something BIG, Simon
Rodia said to Carmen, his wife. There's
no Watts story. Sorry, most sorry.
I'm gonna to do something, said the wee
Italian immigrant, pulling buckles
on his extra-small size overalls. And in
1921, hand-mixed water, gravel
silky sand, he shoveled, anchoring,
cementing detritus towers made of chicken
wire, broken ceramics, found seashells,
dishes. Big Red Cars hummed, vibrated
along rails used to bend scrap steel, refusing
bolts, rivets, and welds. Simon cemented
rocks, discarded tile, slag, 7-Up,
magnesia milk bottle parts. He used lacy,
intricate wire mesh, wrapping towering spires,
walls, and a gilded gazebo into a soaring
explosion of color, form, and texture.
A crescendo of cackling crows, pigeon
wings flapping, mortar-stamped heart-shaped ciphers.

LOOKING BACK...

In addition to Fever, another favorite song of mine is one Sechon introduced me to and played repeatedly: Frank Sinatra's My Way..."/Regrets, I've had a few/ But then again, too few to mention/ I did what I had to do/ And saw it through without exemption.../ Realistically, I've had more than a few regrets and even more opportunities denied. I'm still working on the lines "/ To say the things he truly feels/ And not the words of one who kneels.../ The struggle continues, especially for Black people in America. But I know one thing for certain: I'm less than or second-class to no one. I'll fight the fight and take the blows as necessary for liberty.

Listen to me, baby/Hear every word I say/No one can love you the way I do/'Cause they don't know how to love you my way/You give me fever.

About the Author: Ron L. Dowell
Author / Poet / Community Activist

Ron L. Dowell holds two master's degrees from California State University Long Beach. In June 2017, he received the UCLA Certificate in Fiction Writing. He's a 2018 PEN America Emerging Voices Fellow. His story collection *Crooked Out of Compton* is a semi-finalist in the Chestnut Review Stubborn Artists Contest and a finalist for the Black Lawrence Press 2020 Big Moose Prize. His short story *"Don't Worry"* was a finalist in the 2021 Prime Number Magazine Award for Short Fiction. *"Bruised"* is a Tulip Tree Merit Prize winner. He connects gritty stories showing how people find hope and joy in lives where basic needs are demanding to be met. Ron's stories talk about a suite of sociopolitical realities in an honest, thoughtful way that challenges stereotypes and humanizes people. Running Wild Press' RIZE imprint released *Crooked Out of Compton* on Labor Day, 2024.

Ron's poetry has appeared in Penumbra, Writers Resist, Oyster Rivers Pages, North Dakota Quarterly, The Wax Paper, Kallisto Gaia Press, The Penmen Review, Packingtown Review-Journal, and The Poeming Pigeon. World Stage Press released his *Watts UpRise* collection in July 2022.

crookedoutofcompton.com/
instagram.com/cpt4cops

SIX

IT RUNS IN THE FAMILY

Rona S. Cook-White

1970's

EASY DOES IT

"Now wait, just one god-damn cotton-pickin' minute! Matter-of-fact, get your motherfuckin' ass out my house!" Scrooge roared as he snatched open the front door and more explicatives followed between he and the culprit of his rage until he slammed it shut. He sipped his beer.

"Scrooge! Why you always got to act so ugly? We happy drunks are having a good time, but the miser always gotta show his ass and ruin the party," Suzanne bellowed out in embarrassment as she sipped from her crystal glass filled with Champale, which was like a beer and dry white wine hybrid.

This is a 70's glimpse into one of many parties my mother, Suzanne, and daddy, Scrooge, hosted at our 1,000 sq. ft. 2 bedroom + 1 bath home on the corner of Central Ave and Poplar Street in Compton, CA. It was a pale green bungalow

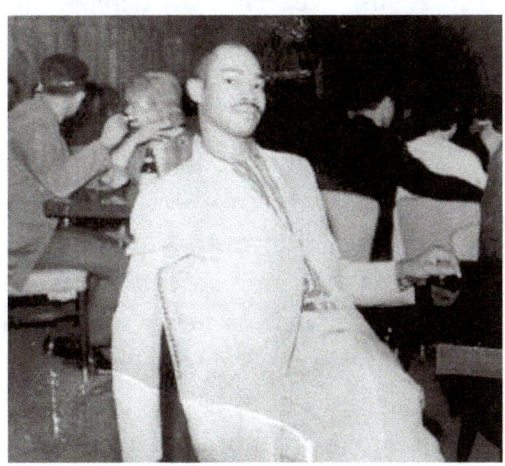

My daddy, Scrooge

style home with aluminum siding. I learned details of these parties as family gathered throughout the years and reminisced on memories full of joy, fun, some gut-wrenching, none-the-less glimpses of shared recalls.

I must address my daddy's name, "Scrooge." He was always, "Daddy" to my sister and I, but everyone else called him Scrooge. It wasn't until I was about 7 or 8 years old when I learned that wasn't

My mother, Suzanne

his real name. I noticed, "Roy" tattooed in cursive on his forearm and searched my memory bank for a family member or friend of his named Roy. The query returned void, but it was a permanent tattoo, so I anticipated my daddy was about to tell me the story of someone important such as a great-grandfather.

Rubbing my finger over the tattoo, I finally asked him "Who's this?"

"That's me! I got this tattoo when I was in Vietnam."

Again, I searched my database to make sense of it and then I got it! "Oh, it's your middle name?"

"No, that's my birthname! I don't know why your mother got everybody calling me Scrooge."

My thoughts sounded something like, "But, you answer to it! Your sisters, brothers, friends, and everyone we know call you Scrooge." However, I didn't share these thoughts. Instead, I suppressed them and accepted what he said.

Even though he never whipped us, he always sounded like he was screaming. Being yelled at was almost as bad as getting a whipping in my book. I never learned how my mother's nickname for him took root, but then again as the saying goes, "Hell knows no fury like a woman scorned."

My daddy was unphased by my mother's charge that he ruined the party. Before things escalated to his temper tantrum, he and some of the guys were hanging out in the Den. It was now vacated but Scrooge settled back into the sofa. He put his beer can down and reached for a long, brown, full-flavored filtered cigarette in a red pack with the brand name, "More" written across it. He put it to his nicotine-stained lips and tightened the grip. After a long, slow pull, inhaling to draw smoke into his lungs, he put the cigarette into an ashtray made of heavy thick transparent green glass.

My mother, Suzanne, and the ladies were back to having a good time lounging in the kitchen. Emptying ashtrays, wiping things down, filling drinks, and cracking jokes was her forte. Their laughter snapped Scrooge off the couch, and he stepped out of the door of the Den which led to the backyard. He could hear family singing "Mississippi Goddam" by Nina Simone in the detached 2-car garage. It was well organized and decorated with drapes he made with his collected beer pull-tabs tied together with small pieces of wire. They were draped over the pedestrian door and large quantity storage areas. They were festive and camouflaged the supplies Suzanne kept in stock for fear of running out of necessities. Scrooge parted the beer pull- tab drapes and percussion sounds like those of wind chimes were made as they clashed together after he stepped inside.

One of his nephews hollered over the music, "Ay Unc, I got your boy Sam Cooke right here and I'll play, 'A Change Gonna Come' right after Nina goes off.

"It's alright, play Marvin Gaye, 'What's Goin' On' or whatever y'all want to hear," Scrooge said as he turned his attention to his youngest brother Tony. "I still can't believe you burned the damn meat. I asked you to watch the pit so I could take a quick break and you didn't lift one damn finger!"

"He lifted his pinky finger each time he took a drink," his nephew chuckled.

"And I looked damn good doing it!" my Uncle Tony said as he dramatically lifted his beer with his long pinky nail extended in

Mother on the phone and me with a wine glass

a ladylike manner.

These were the good ole' days and stories the family often laughed and joked about. You can imagine all the commotion would sometimes wake my sister and I who were toddlers at the time. One of the stories they'd often laugh about was, "I WANT SOME SHITZ!" I would often go to my daddy to get a sip of the beer nestled at the top of his can from the last sip he took. One of my uncle's offered me a sip from his can which was a different brand than my daddy's Schlitz. Not able to properly enunciate words, my answer was, "I don't want that, I want some SHITZ!"

Years later as a young adult sitting in Life Science class at Compton Community College, it would all make sense to me when my instructor explained addiction. I learned there is an "addictive" gene that we all carry which is activated through learned behavior. Just watching my family drink was enough to activate the gene; but being trained to drink beer as a toddler certainly set the stage for addiction to run havoc in my life.

PROGRESSION NOT PERFECTION

In the early 1980s, my sister and I were in elementary school when our parents separated. By this time, "Mommy" changed to "Mother" and Daddy's demons kept him distracted so he was around less and less.

When my mother established the new rule that we were to address her as, "Mother" instead of "Mommy", I resisted for as long as I could. It sounded cold and distant, even though that is what she called her mothers, my three maternal grandmothers. Yes, she had three mothers and we'll get to them in a bit.

She'd always correct me when I called her "Mommy"; so eventually, "Mother" stuck. She probably threatened to "whip" us if we didn't figure it out. I'd heard many parents tell their children, "Go get my belt!" when it was time for a whipping. My mother said, "Go get my Tupperware!" when she was ready to whip our asses. She didn't use a belt to whip us, she used a Tupperware handle from a cake carrier. I suppose she found a good use for it since she wasn't a baker. Most of the time, she whipped us with our clothes on, but there was that one time she kept telling us to get out of the tub. I don't recall the reason my sister and I were in the tub so long together, but I recall the sting of the plastic handle when it hit my bare butt. There was a lingering, burning sensation, and it left raised, triangular welts everywhere the Tupperware handle made contact.

Daddy, on the other hand was "Daddy" 'till the day he died and will forever be Daddy. As mentioned earlier, he never spanked us, but the authority in his voice was enough to keep us in line. He almost always sounded like he was fussing, but it was just the loud country boy in him. I suppose his distractions that kept him away from home could also be blamed on his inner country boy or on learned behaviors from his daddy.

My sister, Purnell, never seemed to care if Daddy was home or not. She was too busy handling her 2nd grader related business.

I'd say, "you think Daddy will be home tonight?"

She often had a flip reply like, "Who cares? It's quiet when he's not here and nobody's arguing!"

When I replied, "they don't argue!" we'd go back and forth.

"They do, too!"

"No, they don't!"

This wasn't a long exchange because it didn't take much for my sister to move on. She'd swiftly change the conversation with something like, "I'm going to kiss my boyfriend!"

Life was so unfair. I was the 4th grader, the older sister, and I should've been the one with a boyfriend. I was supposed to be the first to kiss a boy, not my sister, two years younger than me. All my friends had boyfriends, too. But I looked like my daddy. Adults we hadn't seen in a while would see my sister and I together and say things like, "Purnell, you're so cute! Rona, you look just like your

Me and my sister, Purnell

daddy!" Adults can be so cruel with their damn thoughtless comments. What girl wants to look like her balding daddy while hearing how cute her sister looks?

My sister was light-skinned with "good hair" (also known as curly hair). She was built with the curves of our mother. I was brown-skinned with "nappy hair" (also known as kinky hair). I was built with the lanky limbs of our daddy. Mother didn't have to bother pressing my sister's hair, but she always took the time to straighten mine for special occasions.

So was life. I mentioned my mother had 3 mothers.

Mother #1 – The Humble One:

Her biological mother was raised by strict "God- fearing" parents. She moved away from Virginia to Philadelphia a.k.a. Philly, near two of her sisters after getting pregnant out of wedlock. My mother was conceived during World War II and never knew her father, not even his name. She knew, "he ain't here!" That's what her mother would say whenever she asked about him.

Her mother was a humble woman of few words, but when she spoke, she meant what she said. When Suzanne was 6 years old, her mother had to work nights. In search of a caregiver to watch her young child, she was referred to a community organizer who might have been able to help.

Mother #2 – The Community Organizer, Caregiver

The referred community organizer stayed busy raising a teenage son, organizing women's clubs to include youth services, and she was a fantastic cook. She agreed to add caregiver to her many hats and took the young child in. Within a couple of years, Suzanne spent more time at the home of the caregiver than she did at home with her biological mother.

One day, the caregiver was made aware of terrible news that was happening to Suzanne. Struck with guilt and in a panic to stop the violations that were happening to this young child under her care, the caregiver packed Suzanne up and the two of them moved to Los Angeles for a fresh new start. Suzanne was 8 years old, living in a new state with her second mother, the caregiver.

She spoke on the phone regularly with her biological mother, but they never saw each other again until Suzanne was an adult. Her 2nd mother did her best to make up for the great wrongs that were done to Suzanne back in Philly. After about 6 months, her 2nd mother found in-home employment as a housekeeper, which meant she lived on the premises where she worked. Children were not a part of the employment package. Once again, Suzanne needed overnight care. Her 2nd mother knew of a pianist out of Philly who cared for foster kids in Los Angeles. She reached out.

Mother #3 – The Musician, Foster Mother

That's when Suzanne's 3rd mother came into her life. A musician who taught piano, loved to dance, drank Johnny Walker, and believed in having a good time was happy to add another child to the family. She didn't birth any children of her own but provided a loving home for her 5 foster children. Well, the home was loving, when her drunken husband wasn't beating her ass.

Regardless of any rough Saturday nights, she was always ready for Sunday Mass at the Episcopal Church (Protestant and Catholic mix services) she attended. Suzanne stayed with her foster mother until she was 13 years old when her 2nd mother saved enough money to purchase a home and was able to live off her day job as a cook in a Jewish temple.

Later in life, only one of her kids would grow up with her passion to sing and play piano. None of us grandkids would. It may have had something to do with knuckles and drum sticks during these lessons. If you hit the wrong piano key your knuckles would feel the pain from a drum stick. The drum set sat to the left of the piano.

Scrooge's Childhood Household

Scrooge, on the other hand, grew up in a home with both of his parents and 4 siblings. He was the middle child and was known to have an evil streak. Early life accounts were made about how he once heated a spoon on the stove and put it on his youngest sister's back. She was a toddler, and he was 3 years older than her.

My daddy's "Mama" was a Jesus freak, and his "daddy" was a rolling stone. His mama was the State Mother of Mississippi in the Pentecostal church ministry they were forced to attend with her. She preached at sister churches all over Mississippi and sometimes across the country. She was often away from home leaving their oldest child to care for the kids when they weren't at church with her.

My daddy's "Daddy" drove a taxicab at night. Rumor had it, it was a cover to his extra-marital affairs. When he was home, he'd get so drunk that he couldn't make it outside across the small creak to the outhouse where the toilet was located. Again, their oldest child was leaned on when he'd awake in his living room chair near the couch- bed where the children slept. She had the duty to hold her daddy's "pisser" into the "piss pail" when he was ready to pee. She was 14 when she married to get the hell out of that house. I was a young adult when she shared this horrible childhood task she was burdened with. It left me so distraught I couldn't ask the follow-up questions floating around in my head. It wasn't the last story to leave me horrified.

None of their children attended church as adults. They joked about all the services they had to attend every day of the week, including two on Sundays. Still, I can't help but wonder what else went on in that house that may have led to all the kids turning their backs to the church.

SICK AND TIRED OF BEING SICK AND TIRED

We were at our grandmother #3's home (the musician's home). We kids were in a room where we hung out while the adults drank, played cards, chatted, and partied in the living room. Typically, when it was time to go it would be another hour or so before we actually left so habitually, it wasn't until about the 3rd call to leave when we'd start kissing our grandmother, aunts, and uncles goodbye. It only took one time because the tone in our mother's call this time had us moving like Speedy Gonzales, a cartoon we'd enjoy on Saturday mornings. We rushed out of the room and quickly followed our mother to her sapphire blue station wagon.

Our eclectic grandmother never gave a "classic goodbye." She'd stand on her porch and sing her original tune, "Bye, bye, baby!" This was her signature "good-bye until I see you again" that she belted out until we pulled off.

As we were getting comfortable in our seats our mother gave us odd instruction. "I need you both to get all the way in the back and laydown."

A natural born tomboy, my sister had quickly climbed her small 8-year old body over the backseat and was in the Wayback (the rear compartment of our station wagon) when she asked, "Mother, why do we have to get back here and lay down?"

Meanwhile my 10-year-old mind was still processing the odd command and distressed tone as I crawled my long lanky body over the seat at a snail's pace and met my sister. I had the same question and more; but I already knew the answer, which would shut down any follow-up questions. "Because I said so!" she shouted back in classic Black mama lingo.

We laid down in the back and stared at each other. As the car glided down the street, one of the bounces took my sister's glaze from me. She began meddling around with some surrounding

Tupperware my mother had in the back for some of her clients. I felt a rush of mixed emotions: anticipation, sadness, anger, and determination. I didn't realize then that I was an empath with a supernatural discerning that allowed me to feel the emotions of other people. I eventually learned to suppress this attribute along with many of my own emotions. That's a story for one of my other books.

As the vehicle slowed our mother gave us more instructions, "I'm pulling up at your Uncle Tony's. I want you to keep your heads down. Lay down and don't get up until I come back to get you. I mean it! Do you understand?"

"Yes, Mother," we uttered in unison.

We drove up the alley behind our uncle's duplex when my heart began pounding as we grew closer. My nose was sweating, and my heart was pounding. Suddenly, the car made a loud screech and everything in the car slid forward, including our heads

Uncle Tony on the left and Daddy on the right

as they hit the back of the seats, when my mother slammed on the breaks and muttered something I didn't understand.

Surely, we weren't expected to keep our heads down with this kind of chaos going on. We inched our heads up to peak as she leapt out of her station wagon. Our daddy and Uncle Tony were working on a car in the alley.

Uncle Tony tried to play defense. "Hey, how's my favorite sista-n-law doing?"

It was like my mother was running offense when she swerved around my uncle and threw words at my daddy as she charged like a bull chasing a red cape. I didn't notice her fist come from behind her headed straight for daddy's face but apparently, he did. He caught and cupped it with his hand like a baseball. Next thing I knew, he had both of her arms pinned behind her until she calmed down. Uncle Tony approached, put an arm around her and Daddy let go.

"Hey monkeys! Y'all, c'mon in the house," Uncle Tony called out to us. "Monkey," was an endearing term he called us kids.

Mother looked over at the car window, and we quickly dropped our heads and laid back down. Daddy opened the back of the station wagon.

"Hi girls. C'mon get out this car and give me some shugga." Like nothing happened, we greeted and kissed him as he helped us out of the vehicle.

Daddy escorted us into the duplex, through the living room where our mother was sitting as Uncle Tony consoled her. He took us to the kitchen and said, "Look in the fridge and see if there's a soda pop or something in there you can share" as he headed back outside through a door from the kitchen.

Uncle Tony was my favorite uncle, but I'd soon learn I didn't like being at his home. It was a rare occasion when we went to his residence, and when we did, we typically stayed in the car while the adult we were riding with ran in or Uncle Tony came to the car.

Uncle Tony's house wasn't an ideal spot for kids. This was the first time we went inside. Purnell and I were eager to take advantage of the opportunity to share a soda. Mother didn't allow us to have sweets often, and when she did, we always had to share. She even made us share a piece of gum whenever it was offered to us. She also didn't allow us to drink from cans, so we'd have to find some cups and clean them because so many roaches were crawling around.

We went straight for the fridge. We didn't have high expectations when we opened the fridge but were not prepared for what was on the other side. Roaches! They were alive and crawling on the inside of the refrigerator.

"I didn't know roaches could live inside the refrigerator," Purnell whispered as her eyes followed one that disappeared behind the door. She was intrigued and ready to do further investigation.

"Me neither!" I said repulsed. I quickly closed the fridge and grabbed her hand. "C'mon. Hopefully, it's almost time to go," I continued and led the way back to the living room.

Mother was wiping her eyes as we approached and sat beside her. She wrapped an arm around both of us. Although I was a "Daddy's girl", he was rarely around, and our mother was the one who showered us with love, despite her strict rules and obsessive-compulsive behaviors.

Uncle Tony was sitting on the arm of the sofa across from us. "You know Scrooge is selfish. I don't know why you let yourself get worked up like this."

"I know, Tony. But every time I think about how I'm struggling to pay the bills and put food on the table it just burns me up! While he blows money partying and putting on facades instead of taking care of his responsibilities. He's better off to me ..." she stopped midsentence.

Mother's eyes were fixed on the swords my uncle had leaning against the side of the fireplace. Once again, she switched off safety and like She-Ra, a cartoon warrior we enjoyed watching on TV, our mother grabbed a long-curved sword and began pulling it out of its case. It was beautiful in a white case with details of silver and blue stones.

Now while my mother moved with a quickness, before she could get the sword completely out of the casing, Uncle Tony grabbed Mother's arms and began to talk sense into her. Obviously, this new violent streak wasn't truly who she was, but she was drowning in despair.

Between the roaches crawling all around and the frantic emotions I was absorbing from my mother, along with the threat to kill my daddy, I'd

Mother, Purnell, and me

had enough. Besides, my girl, She-Ra from the cartoon, would've grabbed that sword and stuck my daddy good as she stood over him holding it to his chest until he agreed to do right by us. But this was no cartoon. It was my life, and it was sad.

"Mother, it's time to go home!" I cried with tears welled in my eyes.

She looked at me, her eyes swollen with dark circles and said "Ok, honey. Let's go home."

We were back in the station wagon on our way home. Just the three of us. It wasn't perfect, but it was our normal.

ONE DAY AT A TIME

Most of us can look back on our lives and see pivotal moments or events that greatly impacted or even changed the trajectory

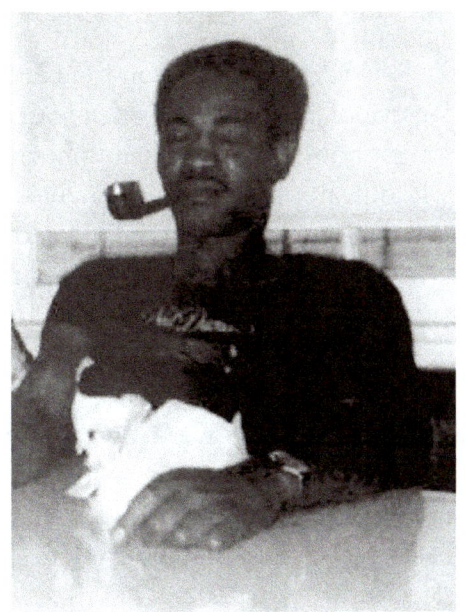

Uncle Tony asleep with a stuffed animal we propped in front of him

of our lives. For my sister, mother, and me, it was one particular night.

Purnell and I were 9 and 11 years old when Uncle Tony came to live with us for a short time. He was such a kid at heart that it was more like having an older brother, at times. Mother was extremely protective of us because of the horrible things that happened to her as a child which led to her move to California. Uncle Tony was the only man who ever lived with us; she didn't allow her boyfriends to sleep over, and she never left us alone with male cousins or uncles. It was likely Uncle Tony's preference for boys/men that kept her at peace. That same fondness is related to the reason he got out of the Army, but that's not my business to tell.

While the months that he stayed with us were fun and

exciting, they were also rather gloomy. He taught us to fight, dance, and the art of negotiation toward the end of the month when he needed money to get a drink. He'd ask us to borrow a few dollars that we'd collect from our piggy banks so he could buy his cheap wine and he'd pay us back 50% – 100% interest depending on our agreement.

Uncle Tony slept on the couch in the den, and when we left for school, he'd climb in one of our beds where we'd find him when we got home. I have a feeling he didn't appreciate my tone when I told him not to smoke in our beds because his ashes were falling and making tiny, burned dots on our blankets. It was probably the next day when he burned a pea-sized hole through the head of my favorite blanket, in the very spot that rested under my chin. That hole served as a reminder of his presence for years after he was gone.

Then there were our parakeets, Tweedy and Daisy. We walked all over the house with them on our shoulders and enjoyed taking care of them. Uncle Tony never took much interest in them besides complaining about them chirping while he was trying to sleep so we started leaving them covered while we were away at school.

One day we came home from school and the birds weren't in their cage. We frantically ran to our room where Uncle Tony was sleeping and asked, "Where are Tweedy and Daisy?"

"I let them outside for some fresh air." "You did what?" we yelled in unity.

"Yea, they're over there in the tree across the street.

Can't you hear them?" he asked.

"Uncle Tony, there's a lot of birds in the tree across the street. Our birds don't know how to care for themselves out there in the wild!" I growled.

"Well, why you standing here talking to me? If you go get them now they should be ready to come in," he insisted.

Of course, we never saw our birds again and we were ready for him to go. We did everything to make him miserable enough to leave. We threw out his cigarettes and poured his liquor down the drain, but he threatened us indirectly, "Suzanne, you betta tell these monkeys something before I hurt 'em!"

Uncle Tony was so angry, and while I don't think we were scared, we definitely took heed to his tone. Mother explained withdrawal symptoms to us and why he needed his cigarettes and alcohol, so we found other ways to annoy him. We'd splash water on him and tickle his nose when he slept; but the best was when he was good and drunk, we'd make him over with Mother's makeup and one day we even took a picture. He didn't care much, but he did promise to buy us another bird and eventually did after he moved out.

Mother didn't drink with Uncle Tony during the week when she had to work, but on the weekends, they stayed good and drunk. She collected crystal and always pulled a crystal wine glass from her yellow bamboo China cabinet to drink her Champale. Mother taught us the proper way to tilt the glass and pour it so there was no collection of carbonation bubbles at the top. As the night grew older, she'd count on us to fill her glass as it got closer to empty. When too many bubbles collected, the conversations went something like this:

"Why didn't you take your time and pour it correctly?" she'd ask.

One of my classic responses was, "I'm sorry, Mother, I'll drink the bubbles for you."

Once I sipped Uncle Tony's cheap wine and it was like I took a swallow of gasoline, so he didn't have to worry about me asking again. When we sipped the bubbles from Mother's Champale, it was never enough for us to get buzzed, but it was just fun for us "monkeys". What wasn't fun was when they'd run low on alcohol and would have to make a "liquor store run." I worried and always wanted to go because it was my way of ensuring she returned home safely.

I was rarely allowed to go with them. One Friday night, they went for a liquor store run and Mother told us to be in bed before they got back. We went to bed but I stayed awake like I always did until she made it back home. Time passed and I was more and more worried, knowing they should've returned home a long time ago. My stomach ached and I kept looking out of my bedroom window hoping to see them pull up.

When I finally heard the chain-link fence close, I felt a bit of relief but when I looked out of my window, I saw Aunt Sis' car. She was my dad's oldest sibling, the one that took care of the rest of the siblings until she got married at age 14 and left the house. She hooked my parents up back when she and my mother worked together. She always looked out for my sister and I and was our biggest advocate.

Aunt Sis opened the door with her spare key. When she came in, she called our names as she approached our room. She turned on the light and said, "I'm going to take you over your grandmother's house to stay the night."

Nothing in that sentence made sense. Why would my daddy's sister be taking us over my maternal grandmother's home? An occasional graduation or birthday maybe, but it was rare to see both of them in the same place at the same time. And why wouldn't Aunt Sis just take us to spend the night at her home? There was no wrapping my mind around this lunacy.

"Why? Where's my mother?" I asked.

"She had to take care of some business, but she's fine and will be home tomorrow."

"Why aren't we going to your home?" I asked.

"I have to help take care of business and that's all you need to know."

The next day, Aunt Sis picked us up from our grandmother's and took us to her aunt's home — our Great Aunt Flo. Again, this was odd. I listened intently for clues, but the adults were careful not to drop any. I had my own theory, and it was the reason I always wanted to go with my mother on her "liquor store runs" when she was already intoxicated.

The next day, Mother came and picked us up! She shared the same story about taking care of important business. I had a pretty good idea what this business involved, but was no longer worried, I was just glad she was home. Uncle Tony on the other hand didn't return, he was still taking care of business.

Monday morning was just like any other except for a small detail. Before she left for work, Mother told us she would be late getting home, so she wanted us to eat dinner without her and clean the kitchen. This routine continued night after night. Mother would get home late and would heat her food in our brand-new *first-ever*, microwave oven that she had recently purchased. It was new technology and before the microwave oven we heated our food on the stove or in the conventional oven.

I'm not sure how I knew what was going on. Perhaps, I'd seen commercials on tv or maybe I saw "The Big Book" lying around. Her Big Book was a large dark blue hardcover book with the title, *Alcoholic Anonymous*, embossed discreetly on the cover with no added color to make the words pop. It is a guide to the 12-step program with testimonials of how the first 100 people of AA worked the program and found sobriety. Today, it is one of the bestselling books of all time, and there are many different versions available, including a free online version.

Regardless of how I knew, my original theory about what happened that night, had developed even further with time. One day, our mother took us to eat at Fiddler's Three Restaurant outside the Carson Mall. She had something to tell us.

"The reason I no longer come straight home from work is because I've been going to Alcoholics Anonymous (AA) meetings."

"I know," I said softly.

"You do? How'd you know?" she asked.

"When you didn't come home that night, I was afraid something bad happened to you but when Aunt Sis said you were fine, I was glad but still worried until you picked us up"

"Yea, it was weird that she took us to Grandmother Ethel's house," my sister added.

I continued, "But then I noticed a pattern when you stopped coming straight home from work. On the weekends you always had somewhere to go for a couple of hours. And you're always on the phone with your new friend. I just put 2 and 2 together and figured that's what was going on." "I'm sorry for worrying you both." Mother continued, "That first night I was arrested for drunk driving. I called your Aunt Sis, and she took care of you two and collected money from the family to bail me out of jail. The judge ordered me to go to AA. I've completed the time that the judge ordered me to do, so I don't have to go anymore. I've learned that I am an alcoholic and going to the meetings helps me stay sober. So I'll keep going back. Going to jail was my rock bottom.

"What's a 'rock bottom'?" my sister asked.

I chimed in, "I know Uncle Tony is an alcoholic, because he drinks all day everyday but you only drink on the weekends."

"And you be throwing up too when you get drunk," my sister blurted.

"I was always afraid that you would get into an accident whenever you would leave to get more Champale," I added.

Mother took it all in and then shared, "I'm what they call a functional alcoholic. It means I can be responsible enough to realize I can't drink during the week, because I might not get up in time to make it to work. But on the weekends, I don't know how to stop. So, it's best for me never to drink alcohol because I would start the cycle all over again."

"Ten and twelve-year-old kids shouldn't be worried about their mother drinking and driving. It took me to be in the powerless position in jail, unable to care for you two, for me to realize that this life was unacceptable. That was my rock bottom. Rock bottom is when you get sick and tired of being sick and tired.

"For me it means I allowed myself to get so out of control that I was no longer the mother that you needed me to be. I couldn't protect you the way I wanted to and that was scary for me just like it was scarry for you not knowing what happened to me when I didn't come home.

They have meetings for you, too. They're called Alateen. I want you both to go."

"Why? Are we alcoholics, too?" my sister questioned. "I don't know. Do you have a stash of liquor I should know about?" she laughed. We all laughed.

"Alateen meetings are kinda like my meetings. Kids are free

to discuss things that bother them," Mother continued. "You'll hear other kids share about what they go through and how they deal with their loved ones using mind altering chemicals. That's what we call drugs and alcohol. It will help you understand and better deal with the alcoholics in your lives."

Mother shared the *Serenity Prayer* with us:

"God grant me the Serenity
To accept the things that I cannot change
The courage to change the things that I can
And the wisdom to know the difference."

LOOKING BACK...

I realize that my mother suffered from PTSD due to the horrible things that caused her to have to move from Philly. To this day, she is like the Energizer Bunny, always moving. I believe it's her way of working off negative energy. She is the epitome of Colossians 3:23, "Plant your seed in the morning and stay busy all afternoon for you don't know if profit will come from one activity or both."

God heard her prayers, and we never experienced the horrible stories that often accompany children raised in this kind of chaotic environment. We were surrounded with love from a bunch of alcoholics and some drug addicts. Together, they protected and loved us unconditionally, because of or despite what they endured.

Alateen provided us an outlet to release the abandonment we felt when our daddy wasn't around, as well as other teenage frustrations. It was therapy at its best, and to this day, we still use some of the clichés in our conversations. If either my sister or I took drinking too far, we could always count on the other to say, "You know the disease runs in the family."

I developed anger management issues which rears its ugly head occasionally, so I use some of the tools I've learned in therapy to address it immediately to avoid a bottleneck explosion. Today, rather than live in fear, I do my best to trust the paths I choose will ultimately lead me through the journey to fulfill my life's purposes for another 50 years here on earth.

About the Author: Rona S. Cook-White
Activist / Author / Entrepreneur / Warrior

As a mother, wife, daughter, sister, friend, author, entrepreneur and encourager, Rona likes to think of herself as a love-caster!

Prior to being diagnosed with lung cancer, she worked in Human Resources Management, as an Educator at a local business college, and enjoyed a journey halfway through a PhD program in Organizational Psychology. As her health challenges grew, her inner warrior emerged even greater. Today, she advocates for greater awareness and increased funding to aid in new therapies for lung cancer and lung health. This is an example of her glass-full perspective and how she finds the good in just about any situation as she wears optimism well. A scripture she lives by is, Proverbs 11:27, "If you search for good, you'll find favor; but if you search for evil, it will find you!"

Her philosophy: "My daughter keeps me young at heart. My husband keeps me protected and warm at night. My mother keeps me humble, and my sister keeps me real. Together with all my friends and family I stay laughing, but most of all, I'm loved and I love to love." Another scripture she lives by, Proverbs 17:22, "Being cheerful keeps you healthy" GNT, or "A cheerful heart is good medicine" NIV. Her mantra, "I will love, live, and laugh; sharing the blessings bestowed upon me as I fulfill each day's purpose with guidance from God!" Psalms 118:17

linkedin.com/in/rona-cook-white/

Great Contributor of the A.C. Bilbrew Black Resource Center: Rose Mitchell

Rose Mitchell is indeed a treasure. Her contribution to the Black Resource Center at A.C Bilbrew Library and to the Los Angeles community is undeniable. Rose is a visionary and an unacknowledged 'Trailblazer.'

Like the late Dr. Mayme A. Clayton (1923-2006), founder of the Western States Black Research Center, Rose recognized the importance of preserving the historical record of an essential aspect of American history. She is the definition of a *public servant*. Her dedicated work is a crucial link in the survival and preservation of this heritage of African Americans.

Rose Mitchell's vast knowledge of the Black experience and Black history put A.C. Bilbrew Library on the map as one of the most resourceful sites in California:

The Black Resource Center developed into one of the more acclaimed Black resource sites in the United States. It is now a world renown Black Resource Center.

The Los Angeles South Chamber of Commerce commended Ms. Mitchell for creating such rich archives. They acknowledged that people travel from all over the world to do research at the Black Resource Center at the Bilbrew Library.

Rose has extended her knowledge to recognize Blacks around the globe, not just the United States. The richness of the Black Resource Center has given the community a sense of pride in that we are celebrated on the world stage.

Ms. Mitchell is one of the first librarians to acknowledge, honor, and celebrate the freedom of the enslaved African Americans at the end of the Civil War. This celebration has become known as Juneteenth.

Ms. Mitchell annually recognized World War II veterans – the Tuskegee Airmen, the first Black aviators in the U.S. Army Air Corps.

Rose encouraged young and old members of the community to participate in Black History Month. She created activities that encouraged everyone to learn more about the richness of their Black heritage.

Ms. Mitchell brought to the community workshops on the Black Seminoles, the Underground Railroad, the art of quilting, African art and so much more.

Rose welcomed workshops from the California African American Genealogical Society.

Ms. Mitchell graciously provided platforms for Black poets and writers to hold classes and workshops for the public.

Rose continued to celebrate and embrace the contributions of Dr. Martin Luther King, Jr. She attended community celebrations and encouraged others to do so.

Rose nurtured the A.C. Bilbrew Writers Workshop and helped maintain ties to the Watts Writers Workshop from the 1960s. She invited a host of notable speakers to the A.C. Bilbrew Library – many the community would not have access to.

Los Angeles County should rightfully rename the Black Resource Center in honor of Rose Mitchell.

Comments from the writers she supported:

Ron L. Dowell – "Rose worked ground-level with aspiring authors and produced book-launch events like mine in 2011 for *Compton4COPS: Community-Based Crime Fighting in Disadvantaged Racially and Ethnically Diverse Urban Communities.*"

Patricia Forté – "I appreciate Rose in that she was always open to any ideas I proposed to her. She respected my opinion and my voice. That meant a lot to me."

Odie Hawkins – ROSE FOR PRESIDENT

I would like to be recognized as the first person in the Bilbrew Writers' Workshop to nominate Rose A. Mitchell, the former head of the Bilbrew Library's Black Resource Center, for President of the International Forum of Black Resources Center, or, as it is popularly called – the I.F.B.R.C.

I'm nominating Rose A. Mitchell for this position because I cannot think of any individual who is better qualified. As a long-time observer of what Rose A. Mitchell accomplished over the course of the years, she was the Director of the Black Resource Center, the diplomatic ways she fused grinding bureaucracies and fast- moving neighborhood dynamics, her ability to discern what the People wanted (needed), plus the groove she created.

For these reasons and many more, too numerous to mention here, I think that Rose A. Mitchell would be the ideal President to offer the International Forum of Black Resources Center. And, if there is no such organization presently in existence, then funds should be allotted to allow Rose A. Mitchell to create one. I cast my vote and rest my case.

Zola Hawkins – Rose A. Mitchell is the kind of librarian I wanted to be when I graduated from Hackensack High School, Hackensack, New Jersey. I realize now that if I had become a librarian, I never would be able to be the extraordinary person she is. On an average day/week, a librarian is required to manage books, periodicals, audio and video recordings, digital resources including cataloging, dealing with the internal needs for storage at the facility. Librarians assist individuals with research regarding appropriate databases or books for such research. Then, they must oversee the use of the materials, so they don't disappear from the library. The most difficult thing, I believe, is dealing with difficult people. Rose A. Mitchell can do all of this and more. She reminds me of an employee that handled so much themselves; and when they retired the company had to hire two people to do that job. There is no way she can be replaced because she is the Super Woman she is. I hope she enjoys her retirement at least as much as we have enjoyed having her in our lives.

Rona White – "Rose has always been a great resource, a beautiful guiding light. When I shared with Rose my love for writing and the stories I'd written and those I had yet to have written, she walked me over to the Bilbrew Writers' Workshop meeting and introduced me to the legendary Odie Hawkins."

Eddie White – "Rose was always friendly, warm, helpful, and kind towards me. She encouraged me to continue with my poetry. She said my voice needed to be heard. Rose will always be known as the librarian with a heart for the community."

Jillian Kaufman – "I have known Rose for years. She was the librarian who helped me with issues I had on the computer. We struck up a friendship and Rose helped me become a reader for the young children's group at the library. Because of Rose I gained much confidence as the reader for my group (3-6 years). I thank her for that."

Cheryl-Greer-Davis – "Rose was a soft-spoken giant in African American literacy. She was knowledgeable, resourceful, and a beacon of light for those who needed information regarding the African American experience. Rose empowered us to embrace our heritage and to dig deeper to learn what we contributed to the American blueprint. As an educator, Rose understood my needs. Whenever I came to her, she appreciated what I was doing for the students. I enjoyed coming to the library because I knew Rose would take good care of me. When she retired, she took a part of us with her! We will miss you, Rose."

Charles Chatmon – "Rose had always been there when I needed her. She helped and assisted me with the Bilbrew Writers' Workshop from 2005-2018. She helped me tremendously in coordinating the last L.A. Black Book Expo in the Bilbrew Library when space was no longer available. Rose has meant so much to me personally. I will forever be indebted to her. She has shown her willingness to help me in any way she can. Thank you, Rose."

About the Editor: Flo S. Jenkins
Editor / Writer-Ghostwriter / Teacher

Flo Jenkins has an extensive communications background with a successful career including major media industries — i.e., *television* (KTLA), *recording industry* (Arista Records), and *publishing* (Laufer). As a writer and executive editor, she popularized the nation's first #1 Black teen magazine (*Right On! Magazine*) and helped spotlight and enliven many notable careers, including the Jackson Five, the Sylvers, Al Green, along with writing about/ generating interest in Black interests overall – movies and tv shows, including popularizing Don Cornelius's successful *Soul Train* and its multi-talented dancers. She has written for major influencers like Johnson Publishing and others. Flo's writing/editing/PR skills have supported local and global industries, including Saatchi & Saatchi, the Act One Group and more. Ms. Jenkins was recruited as Executive Editor/Spokesperson for nationally-renown Crenshaw Christian Center (Dr. Frederick K. C. Price, III) where she wrote/edited all materials including brochures and the monthly newsletter, managed a staff of 5, and was named *Editor of the Year*.

Flo established her own company, Words That Flo! ... Editorial Consultancy Services and GoodJenks Publishing Group, Inc. nearly 20 years ago to provide professional writing-editorial support for individuals (authors, company execs, medical, educational community, etc.). A skilled speaker-teacher and former college writing instructor, Flo Jenkins also taught a special writing program in Compton, California for elementary school children. She continues to teach writing through her *How to Get Published* personal seminars and her *Telling Our Stories Ourselves Worldwide* workshops series mainly for African Americans—including senior citizens, teens, and pre-teens.

Flo Jenkins is also a poet and published playwright (*First Piece/Peace*) performed at local colleges and throughout Southern California. She has authored 3 books including *Telling Our Stories Ourselves; Hello, My Name is Erma...and I Matter; I Think. I Feel. I Write*. She is a documentarian and historian whose work reflects the impact of Black- African American History and its effects primarily on the 1970s – through today's culture. She is the proud mother to 3 adult millennials, all making positive impacts on their generation *and* the world in their chosen fields.

www.wordsthatflo.com
goodjenksmedia@gmail.com

A Moment in Time: Meet the Authors

Watch these videos to learn more about the Bilbrew Writers' Workshop members.

Jerry Boyd

Patricia Forté

Odie Hawkins

Zola Salena-Hawkins

Ron L. Dowell

Rona S. Cook-White